SPALDEEN DREAMS:

A Boy Comes of Age in 1950's Brooklyn

By James Pantaleno

INTRODUCTION

Oh how the world has changed.

In the 1950's, I grew up in what we believed to be a middle-class section of Brooklyn called East New York. Actually it was poor, but we never knew it. Most families on my block and in the surrounding areas were in similar circumstances. Fathers worked in small jobs for little money. Because of this, many worked a second job to give their families the few small luxuries they craved. Mothers stayed at home and raised the children. Some did odd jobs like babysitting or took in sewing to make a few extra dollars. We kids grew up in the streets with so much more freedom than kids have today. With little in the way of material things, we were forced to make up our own games and enforce the rules.

Many of these games were played with a pink, high-bounce ball made by the Spalding Company. For some unknown reason, Brooklyn kids pronounced it "Spaldeen". The Spaldeen was a big part of my childhood. My friends and I spent endless hours playing with this little ball while dreaming of becoming the next Joe DiMaggio or Jackie Robinson. Any kid who could hit a Spaldeen "two sewers" was among the first picked when we chose up sides for stickball.

I guess those "Spaldeen Dreams" never came true for most of us, but along the way we were creating wonderful memories of growing up in Brooklyn during the 1950's. I read where one in seven Americans can trace their roots back to Brooklyn. And if you asked them, I'd bet not many would choose to trade their childhood on the streets of Brooklyn for any other place in the world. I was surrounded by family and extended family. Holiday dinners with the whole clan are among my most cherished recollections of that time.

It was a time before computers, cell phones, and video games. Not everyone had a telephone and ever fewer had televisions. We had radios, comic books, vinyl records and board games for entertainment. We rode old bikes, roller skates and scooters to get around. The neighborhood was filled with Mom and Pop stores where they knew you and added up your purchases with a pencil on the side of a brown paper bag. People looked out for one another. Every kid on the block had ten mothers and if you did something wrong, your mother knew about it before you got home.

In short, it was a wonderful time to grow up. Let me tell you about it.

DEDICATION

I never fully appreciated how much my parents did for me until it was too late.

Most Italian-American sons will, at some time in their lives utter these words: "My mother was a saint!" In my case it was true. My mother, Frances Camardi Pantaleno, was the most unselfish woman I ever knew. She had a way of making me feel safe and loved. She habitually gave up material things for herself so her three children might have a little more. She taught us by the way she lived her life. Fran always saw the good in people even when it wasn't always there. My father's mother lived with us and did her best to make my mother's life miserable. My mother endured her. She always put herself last and we let her. Shame on us.

My father, Anthony Pantaleno, was known around the neighborhood as "Tony Boots" because he held down a second job at the A.S. Beck shoe store on Pitkin Avenue. Tony was a good time guy who liked a drink and a joke. He was always teasing Mom about being a "Killjoy" because she had the tough job of trying to keep him from investing in every crazy scheme that came down the pike. She was Alice to his Ralph Kramden. My dad wore suits and ties pretty much every day of the week. He was the least handy guy I know but could sweet talk our neighbor Frank into doing jobs for him around the house. I think I get my sense of humor from my father, and for that I am grateful.

When I was dating I naturally used my Mom as a yardstick. I wanted a girl just like the girl that married dear old Dad. And after some false starts, I found her. Jasmine is the best partner anyone could ask for. Besides being beautiful inside and out, she has the temperament, patience and forgiving nature to love me in spite of my faults. Because of her I went to college at night while she raised three kids. She encouraged me in my career and was there to make my failures bearable. My feelings for her can be expressed in a quote from the movie, "As Good As It Gets" spoken by Jack Nicholson to Helen Hunt: "You make me want to be a better man." I am nothing without her.

Finally, a shout-out to my best friend, Rich Bilello. We have shared a million laughs over the 70 years I know him. Besides being everything a guy could want in a friend, Rich introduced me to my wife. I could never repay that. Also, he has been encouraging me to write this book for a long time now, so Rich, I finally got off my ass and did it.

Thank you all.

NOTES

Except for family members and a few friends, I have tried to change the names of people I remember from real life for privacy reasons.

My recollections I believe are fairly accurate. If I got anything factually incorrect, it was unintentional. Although I tried to avoid it, these essays were written over time, so there may be some overlap.

The photos used here are old and not of the best quality and I apologize for that. The content of these essays and photographs may not be used elsewhere without my written permission.

TABLE OF CONTENTS

I gave a lot of thought to how to organize this book and finally came to the conclusion that it does not lend itself to organization. Most of these essays were written at random, and that's how they are presented here. I hope you enjoy them.

TABLE OF CONTENTS (CONTINUED)

TABLE OF CONTENTS (CONTINUED)

TABLE OF CONTENTS (CONTINUED)

TABLE OF CONTENTS (CONTINUED)

SPALDEEN DREAMS:

A Boy Comes of Age in 1950's Brooklyn

By James Pantaleno

77a Somers Street in Brooklyn where I grew up

Chapter 1: BEGINNINGS

On July 5, 1942 I was born to Frances and Anthony Pantaleno in Unity Hospital on St. John's Place in Brooklyn. We lived in a rented apartment on Pacific Street down the block from Our Lady of Loreto Church where I was baptized.

Our Lady of Loreto was built by Italian immigrants in 1908 on the corner of Sackman and Pacific Streets in the Brownsville section of Brooklyn. Masses were said in Italian and English back in the day. It was a decidedly blue-collar congregation. On Sunday mornings the pews were filled with sunburned men who worked with their hands during the week. They looked uncomfortable in their good suits and shined shoes but wouldn't think of coming to church unless they dressed properly.

Next to them were their wives who worked just as hard around the house in the days before modern conveniences. They wore well-mended dresses and maybe a saucy new hat on special days like Easter Sunday. The children wore clean clothes and hand-me-down shoes; their skin almost shone from being scrubbed. These descendants of immigrants were the backbone of post-war Brooklyn. That church was the center of their religious and social life…Christenings, communions, confirmations, graduations, weddings and finally funerals.

The community turned out in droves for the church's street feasts that featured food, games of chance, and music from men playing songs from the old country on an assortment of battered instruments. Younger men paraded up the street carrying the statue of Our Lady of Loreto decorated with streamers of money donated by the faithful. But slowly, the neighborhood changed and the congregation diminished. The Brooklyn Archdiocese announced intentions to tear down the church. Parishioners fought to keep it going but in 2017 it came down.

The church may be gone, but will always live on in the memories of those who worshiped there.

My father Anthony (Tony Boots) and me on the stoop of our first apartment on Pacific Street.

Chapter 2: SOMERS STREET

When I was about two years old we moved to our new home on Somers Street. This was my parents' first house and the one where I spent my childhood. It was a brick row house, not elegant enough to be called a brownstone, but a substantial structure. There were three floors and a cellar. We occupied two floors: the first, also referred to as the "parlor" floor, and the second, where our bedrooms were located. The third floor was a rental apartment where my cousin Pete and his family lived.

The entry to the house was up a couple of steps from the sidewalk. By today's standards the kitchen was primitive. The stove and refrigerator were born in the Truman administration, although later on we got a new washing machine but no dryer. We ate at a green Formica table. Off the kitchen was the parlor/living room featuring a sofa, Archie Bunker style chair, a "hi-fi" record player and our RCA 17" black and white TV. There was also a fake fire place where we hung our Christmas stockings. (As a kid, I always wondered how Santa came down from the chimney since there was no opening.)

The master bedroom where my parents slept was upstairs at the rear of the house overlooking the tiny back yard. My sister's room was next to theirs, and at the front of the house, looking out on the street was the room where I slept. I can remember on hot summer nights turning my bed around so that my head was nearly out the open window. In all the years we lived there, I never remember getting downstairs ahead of my mother. She had the coffee pot on and made a number of trips up the stairs trying to wake my father, who always needed "just another five minutes".

The cellar was my sanctuary. On cold or rainy days I would spend hours playing cowboy. My Aunt Anna had fashioned a "horse" out of an old narrow table. She sewed on an upholstered saddle and made a head out of an old rug. I would tear off strips of newspaper and stick them in the crevices of the limestone cellar walls as if they were dynamite fuses. I'd light the fuses and then make a leaping mount onto my horse. (This activity may help explain the higher-than-normal pitch of my voice today.) The cellar was also where I would make my street scooters out of wooden fruit crates and roller skates. My father wasn't really a handy guy, and his tools were not much further advanced than those used by the Pilgrims, but I managed.

My memories of this house are warm. Surrounded by aunts, uncles, cousins, grandparents and friends, I cannot imagine a happier childhood, and I will be forever grateful for having the good luck to be raised there.

My Dad with my sister Cathy and me in the front yard.

Chapter 3: FRANCES

I wrote briefly about my mother Frances earlier, but wanted you to know her a little better. I referred to her as Saint Frances because to me she epitomized goodness. She didn't go around making a show of helping others; it was just in her nature. In moving through life, she gave everybody consideration before she thought about her own wants and needs. She went out of her way to see the good in people. If you asked her: "Fran, what do you think about Hitler?" my mother's reply would probably be: "I hear he was a good dancer!"

Like all good Saints, her life was not easy. She hated asking for help, and would personally do any job that needed doing, even if it meant less sleep or time for herself. I can't remember her ever sitting down with a book. When television came into our home, she indulged herself by watching a few of her favorite shows. Fran loved to laugh, and would look forward to The Jack Benny Show, I Love Lucy, and The Danny Thomas Show. We would usually watch with her. Sitting on that couch laughing together was a simple act; who could have imagined it would bring back such warm memories.

My Dad's pet name for her was "Killjoy" because she often had to rain on some of his more impulsive schemes. My father was always on the lookout for a tip on a hot stock or a fast horse. Of course, the minute Tony got on board, the stock cooled and the horse died! Mom did not enjoy this role, but soon realized that somebody in the family had to show some common sense. Tony teased her mercilessly about all the things she would not let him do, but probably if not for her squirreling away some secret cash, the bills would have gone unpaid.

Mom was the quintessential Italian mother without the negatives. She never tried "guilting" us into doing something; we knew this, and somehow her restraint caused us to do exactly as she wanted. She could take scraps of food normally thrown away and whip them into a meal to die for. Without being told, she *knew* when we were hurting. She wouldn't speak directly to us about our problems; that wasn't her way. She would just make herself available to us in a quiet moment, and we would blurt out whatever was on our minds.

She never worked at a "job" until late in her life. God knows caring for three kids (four if you count my father) and also my grandmother Lucia (don't ask) was enough of a job for anyone. I guess the extra money came in handy. I think just as important to Mom though was to feel needed. With her children grown, she got a job in a school cafeteria and really enjoyed going to work. She liked being around kids again. She also volunteered at a local nursing home. I had occasion to talk to the director of the home years after my mother worked there. She remarked that she remembered my mother well, and said she was one of the best volunteers they ever had. I can't say I was surprised

Regrettably, I did some dumb things growing up. I can imagine my poor mother making countless novenas praying for her directionless son. I think she would have been happy if I got a steady job selling tube socks out of my car trunk. When I finally straightened out, got a real job, and married my wife Jasmine (who my mother adored), probably no one was more surprised or pleased than Fran. I wish she could have lived to see her three grandchildren grow up.

In the "me first" world we inhabit today, Saint Frances would stand out like a sore thumb. She always saw the glass half-full, made lemons into lemonade, and made you feel like there was no hurt in the world that in her quiet way, she couldn't somehow make a little better. As if being the very soul of goodness on the inside wasn't enough, you can tell from the photo of her as a young girl that she was beautiful as well. Saint Frances was quite the complete package. I only wish I could have grown up to be more like her.

Chapter 4:   ANTHONY

Anthony (Tony Boots) came to America from southern Italy at the age of 2 with his parents and older brother, Joe in 1912. He never had the luxury of an education. His own father died young, so Tony and Joe both worked from an early age to help support the family. He married in 1940 and set up house on Pacific Street. I never remember my father wearing anything but a suit and tie, and of course his snappy fedora. He worked a series of unglamorous jobs including a second part-time job as a shoe salesman at A.S. Beck on Pitkin Avenue.

My dad was the least handy guy I know. If there was any serious work to be done, he would sweet talk our neighbor Frank into doing it while dad provided the beer and the conversation. He made some of the worst real estate deals in Brooklyn history, always selling at the wrong time. His bad luck carried on to the racetrack where he liked to take a flutter when he could get away. Tony loved nothing more than to sit in a local bar having a few beers and telling jokes. His signature move was to elbow you in the ribs when he delivered the punch lines. Everyone knew his jokes by heart, but he enjoyed telling them so much, they laughed every time.

I never really appreciated how hard my father worked to give us what we had in life. He and my mother always put themselves last, and pushed their children to go to school so they might have a better life. I'm ashamed to say there were times as a kid when, in my youthful arrogance, I considered him a failure. Mark Twain has a wonderful quote about his feelings toward his father, which perfectly mirror my own:

"When I was a boy of fourteen, my father was so ignorant I could hardly stand to have the old man around. But when I got to be twenty-one, I was astonished at how much the old man had learned in seven years."

Thanks Tony for being the father I am always trying to become.

Frances and Anthony (Tony Boots)

My parents wedding, September 29, 1940

Chapter 5: OUR NEIGHBORS

The Ruthefords

The Rutherfords lived in the house to our left, and always seemed a bit out of place. They were of English descent, (already an anomaly on my block) and they could have come from central casting as the prototypical English family. The family included parents David and Ellen, their children, Richard and Victoria, and two spinster aunts...we called them Aunt Peg and Aunt Helen. David was the image of a proper Brit....very distinguished looking, tall, slim, a thin mustache, rimless glasses, and always dressed like a banker. In fact, he did work in a bank. Ellen could have doubled for Jane Wyatt from the old "Father Knows Best" TV show. She was pretty, vivacious, nicely dressed, and I had a huge crush on her.

The two prize characters in the family were Aunt Peg and Aunt Helen. They could have stepped out of the cast of the movie: "Arsenic and Old Lace".. Always beautifully dressed and powdered, they exuded refinement. Occasionally, they would invite me into the house (after locking up the silver) and offer me a piece of fruit or candy. I imagine they felt some sense of "noblesse oblige" to those in the neighborhood like me who were lower born. I tried to be polite (their appearance demanded nothing less) but honestly I couldn't wait to bolt out the door. In my own urchin way, I felt somehow unworthy to be in their presence. I thought of them years later, while watching the wonderful movie, "My Fair Lady"; naturally I identified strongly with Liza Doolittle.

The spinster sisters had a "Gentleman Caller" whose name was "Mr. Winter", and that's how we always addressed him. He too was regal in bearing and impeccably dressed in a three-piece pinstripe suit, white shirt and silk tie. He would unfailingly tip his homburg hat whenever he greeted you. Mr. Winter drove an immaculately kept, tan-colored Chevrolet that looked like it had never seen a spec of dirt. Most weekends he would drive up and take Aunt Peg and Aunt Helen for drives in the country. As incongruous as this scene may sound for a blue-collar Brooklyn neighborhood, it was just accepted.

The Rutherfords were part of the varied ethnic and racial fabric of East New York, Brooklyn in the fifties. We had diversity, but weren't sanctimonious or self-congratulatory about it. We were all neighbors just trying to get by.

The Simeones

To our right lived the Simeone Family.

The ground floor was occupied by Grandma and Grandpa Simeone. He was a man with a face grizzled from the sun and tufts of white hair sticking up from his head. He was on in years and often sat in the front yard on a bench under a Weeping Willow tree smoking his pipe and keeping an eye on the block. One of Grandpa Simeone's hobbies was making homemade wine. Every year he had boxes of grapes delivered by the truckload and had them brought down to the cellar to be turned into red wine that was drinkable only if you mixed it with cream soda.

The middle floor was occupied by Delores Simeone and her husband Joe. On the he top floor lived Frank and Frances Simeone, two of the sweetest neighbors anyone could ask for. Frank was a big man who reminded me of the actor James Arness. Frank was my father's go-to guy when there was a job he couldn't handle. Their children were Barbara, Philip and Loretta. Phil was a year older than me and we became lifelong friends. Like his dad, Phil was a big, good-looking guy who was also a great dancer thanks to watching American Bandstand.

Whenever we went to church dances, we used Phil as bait to attract all the pretty girls who wanted to dance with him. We survived on his leftovers. Phil went on to become a Franciscan Brother who distinguished himself as a teacher and eventually became their Director of Vocations. Later in life he left the Order, married and now lives in Phoenix, Arizona with his wife Susan and daughter Claire.

I am blessed to have a friend like him. I miss seeing him every day.

The Simeone Family (Phil, Frances, Frank, Loretta, Barbara

Phil Simeone, stud

Chapter 6: OUR LADY OF LOURDES CHURCH

Our Lady of Lourdes Church was one of the most stunning churches in Brooklyn. It was in the Bushwick section of the borough on Aberdeen Street. The church was a magnificent structure that featured a Grotto behind the altar that recreated the appearance of Mary to some children at a cave in France. I was baptized nearby at our Lady Of Loreto, but when we moved to Somers Street. Lourdes became our parish.

During the 1950's, this was a thriving congregation that was heavily Irish. There were at least six full-time priests assigned to the parish along with some weekend associates. (This level of staffing is unheard of in today's Catholic churches.) There was a grade school where boys and girls were separated. The boys were taught by lay teachers up to fourth grade and by Franciscan Brothers from fifth grade to eights. The girls were taught by the Sisters of St. Joseph for all eight years. There was no kindergarten yet.

The church was very well attended. They had a full schedule of Sunday and daily masses. The church was a large one, and to fill it was a testament to the faith of the people in the parish. Midnight Mass at Christmas was a sellout. Tragically, in 1976, arsonists torched the church and it had to be torn down. The school remained for many years after that, but with the church gone and demographic changes happening in the neighborhood, the parish was never the same.

Chapter 7: OUR LADY OF LOURDES SCHOOL

I attended Our Lady of Lourdes School in Brooklyn. No pre-K, no Kindergarten, just bam, first grade, cold turkey. Our teacher was Miss Langley, an elderly woman who looked like she stepped out of a Tennessee Williams play. She died shortly after we finished first grade. All the kids were required to attend her wake at the funeral home directly across from the school. This was probably the first funeral any of us had attended. As we lined up to view the body, we tried to cover up our nervousness by joking around, as scared young boys will do. She looked so peaceful in a lovely, pale-blue dress. I left my first encounter with death thinking Miss Langley looked better than she ever did in life.

Parochial school was a no-nonsense affair. If you misbehaved, it was dealt with swiftly by the lay teachers who taught us through grade 4, and the Franciscan Brothers who taught grades 5-8. Nuns taught the girls in separate classrooms. Once another boy and I were carrying a plaster statue of Jesus into the 8th grade girls' room. As we shuffled slowly into the room trying to keep the statue from falling, I tripped over the bench seat of a desk that had been left folded down. The statue hung in mid-air for a split second before shattering into a thousand pieces.

Sister Mary Richard had a look of unspeakable horror on her face and was momentarily frozen like the rest of us. She recovered quickly though and proceeded too beat the hell out of me, all five feet of her. Another time Brother Francis hung me from my belt on a hook in the "cloak room" (that's a coat room to those of you under 70) until he felt I had learned my lesson. Today, kids get teary-eyed at the idea of having to learn script writing. If you ask them to write: "I will not chew gum in class" 100 times, it's considered "corporal punishment". Geez.

Around third grade we made our First Communion. Boys wore stylish outfits like the one I'm modeling in the picture, while girls wore white dresses with veils. Today First Communion parties are elaborate affairs costing more than my wedding. For my First Communion, I cleared around ten bucks and felt giddy with riches. For Confirmation a few years later, boys dressed more conservatively in dark blue suits. My mother dragged me to Klein's Department Store in Union Square to buy a suit. She made sure it was "big enough" to last me a few years. (Mom, you'll be happy to know that the suit would fit me to this day!)

Some people might think we were treated horribly, but I never felt that way. Class sizes were 40 to 50 and even public schools used strict discipline back then. I think we came away with a sound education. I don't envy teachers today having to deal with unruly kids and helicopter parents.

Me in first grade

Me at First Communion

Chapter 8: CHALK DUST ANGELS

I want to say a few words about the women who taught us in the younger grades. There was no kindergarten when I went to school in The Middle Ages; having been born in July, I was one of the younger kids in the class when, at age 5, I entered first grade in September, 1947. Today I might have been held back because of the *"trauma"* of being in class with more mature five-year olds. Luckily, they didn't worry about psycho-babble like this in those days; my mother just hitched up the buckboard and took me off to school.

Our Lady of Lourdes was typical of parochial schools in Brooklyn. The classrooms looked pretty much alike, with orderly rows of old-style wooden desks that had holes cut out for *ink wells* in the top. The little bench seats folded down, and there was a small shelf underneath the desk for storing books not in use. The learning environment could be described as very regimented and very disciplined, but man did it work. In a match between a bright, 1950 eighth-grader from Lourdes versus a high school senior from almost any current New York City graduating class, my money would be on the kid from Lourdes.

I have already written about Miss Langley in first grade. For the first six months of second grade we had the lovely Miss Ruffalo, daughter of Dr. Ruffalo and a pleasant change from Miss Langley. She was dark and pretty, and treated us like humans. We all responded by falling madly in love with her. Imagine our horror when we returned from Christmas break to find out she was having a baby, and there would be someone to replace her! We were crestfallen; who could take Miss Ruffalo's place. When we met her replacement, Miss Theiss, we were dumbstruck. She was a cool, shimmering, Grace Kelly look alike with a smile that turned you to mush. We were like the kids in that episode of the "Our Gang" comedies when they feared that their new teacher, Miss Crabtree, would turn out to be an ogre *until they saw her*. Needless to say, we quickly recovered and instantly forgot old Miss Whatshername.

Third grade...back to boot camp. After six months with the heavenly Miss Theiss, we ran smack into *Tug Boat Annie*, otherwise known as Miss Wall. She was a lean, mean fighting machine who was not afraid to rule with an iron fist. By the way, that's not a metaphor; she literally had an iron fist! If you needed to stand for a while in the dark coat closet because you didn't know the capital of North Dakota, she would grab you by the hair of your sideburns and lead you there. (This technique was later picked by the Nazis and used effectively in interrogations of Allied prisoners.) If you did something really bad, say like making the well-known, rude underarm noise, she would stand you in front of the blackboard, grab your two jug ears, and pound your head against the board. Crude but effective; kids studied like never before to avoid getting left back for another year with the Iron Maiden.

Finally, there was Miss Bauman in fourth grade. We simply adored her, not because she was beautiful (she was not), but because she somehow had the God-given power to tame the little beasts that we were without ever lifting a finger. We wanted her approval in the worst way and would do anything, *even study*, to get it! We would line up in the pouring rain outside her house down the street from the school, hoping, praying, that our umbrella would be the one she chose to walk under! If she asked you to clap the erasers and wash the blackboards, you were in ecstasy. If I had to make a guess as to what mysterious power she had over us, I would say it was her incredible serenity. She never raised her voice, and she had this Mona Lisa smile that, when she turned it on you, made you feel like you were the best person the world had ever produced.

These wonderful women, working for less than a living wage, dedicated their lives to educating street urchins. Whether they hit, hollered, smiled, cajoled or charmed, they somehow knocked and ironed the rough edges off us until we were fit to be among civilized people. I never appreciated how much they did for me until I realized that the seeds of learning they sowed would continue to flourish throughout my life. I thank them, and tip my hat to teachers everywhere.

Typical class at Our Lady of Lourdes. This was fifth grade with Brother Mathias

Our Lady of Lourdes School   6th Year   1953-54

Chapter 9: STREET GAMES

As a kid I remember toys having a season. Everyone played with a particular kind of toy for a while and then moved on to something else. We didn't plan it, it it just happened that way. For a while it was wooden tops. Everybody walked around with a top and string in his pocket. Usually you learn to spin a top by throwing it underhand. The best top spinners though, the ones who could split other kids' tops in half, were the kids who threw overhand like a baseball with great force and accuracy.

Then one day, suddenly marbles were in. You could buy marbles cheaply enough at the candy store, but it was more fun to win them from other kids. There were jumbos, peewees and purees. One marbles game involved carving a "shimmy" (hole) out of the street asphalt near the curb. There were rules in marbles. If something in the gutter like a popsicle stick blocked your shot at another marble, you were allowed to take a "roundsies" to move your shooting marble around the obstacle, but no closer to your target marble.

How about carpet guns? Talk about dangerous. We'd cut up maybe inch square pieces of old linoleum and shoot them at each other with wooden carpet guns we made from old fruit crates. Rubber bands were stretched tight on the gun, the ammo was loaded, and when the rubber band was released the linoleum square would come sailing wildly through the air. If you hit anything with one of these guns, it was purely by accident. "You'll shoot your eye out!" our mothers would say.

Homemade street scooters are maybe my favorite. An old fruit crate served as the top attached to a two by four board to which an old roller skate, split in half, had been nailed at either end. Sometimes we nailed two pieces of wood to the top of the crate to steer the scooter. Also, any kid worth his salt decorated his scooter with bottle caps and painted it to look cool. We raced these in the street because the sidewalks were too rough and your teeth would rattle from the vibrations.

Everything we played with had one thing in common…it cost next to nothing! Besides the pink "Spaldeen" ball for 10 cents, we had pea shooters, yo-yos, water pistols, baseball cards, the paddles with the little red ball attached by an elastic, kites, comics, cap guns, roller skates, beat-up bikes with playing cards in the spokes…life was never ever boring. Best childhood ever.

Chapter 10: BASEBALL

For me as a kid, Spring meant one thing above all else...baseball. We played football and roller hockey in the streets in the winter, but to me that was like just killing time until it got warm enough to suit up and take the field. I remember playing for our grammar school team under the watchful eye of coach John Bryan. We practiced mostly in Highland Park on Jamaica Avenue, where left field sloped severely upward, and anything hit deep to left was tough for a fielder to run down because he was running uphill. Luckily I played center field where the ground was more level. We played some of our games there too, or at the Parade Grounds in beautiful Prospect Park. That's me top left with all the hair. Sigh.

Sometimes I'll be walking by a baseball field today and hear that unmistakable crack of the bat. The sound transports me back in time to hot, sunny days where you could literally smell Spring in the air. We'd stand around the enclosed chain link cage waiting our turn to take batting practice. While we waited it was customary to hurl brutal insults at whoever was unlucky enough to be at the plate. The hitter would glower at his tormentors, trying even harder to hit one over the fence to shut us up. This pressure to hit one hard usually led to strikeouts, prompting gales of laughter from the jeering chorus and much colorful swearing from the hapless batter.

When fielding practice came along, the infielders were drilled in scooping up ground balls and making that long throw to first base. Outfielders practiced shagging fly balls hit by the coach, and firing the ball in to home plate to simulate throwing out that runner who had the nerve to challenge your arm. Although a lifelong Yankee fan, I modeled myself after the great Dodger right fielder, Carl Furillo. Carl was renowned in the National League for having a "gun" for a throwing arm, and not many runners put his reputation to the test. For my entire baseball career, I always wore number 6 on my uniform as a tribute to Furillo.

When we weren't playing on a baseball field, it was stickball in the street. If you think it's easy having a ball game in the middle of a city street, try it sometime. There were mutually agreed upon rules about what happened if a car came down the block while play was in progress. It was the only way to manage, but we were resourceful city kids and we made it work. We'd saw off the handle from some poor family's broom to use for a bat until we found a broom factory that would sell us new broomsticks in bright red or blue for just ten cents. All we needed was a Spaldeen and the game was on. We used car fenders and manhole covers for bases, and after the game, no matter the outcome, it was ice cold sodas at the candy store for everybody.

The great baseball player Rogers Hornsby said: "People ask me what I do in winter when there's no baseball. I'll tell you what I do. I stare out the window and wait for spring." That's a little how I felt growing up. I remember laying down in the outfield smelling the new grown grass mingled with the smell of my oiled leather glove. It was an amazing time when nothing ached and my energy was boundless. When I get that first whiff of Spring, I am standing in shallow center field with the sun hot on my neck, just daring someone to hit one over my head. Of course all of this is in my mind. My body is worn down now, and I sympathize with comedian Ray Romano who recently commented that he's so out of shape that he pulls a muscle doing a Rubik's Cube.

Our Lady of Lourdes Baseball Team

I wore uniform number 6 in honor of Carl Furillo

Chapter 11: THOSE WHO CAME BEFORE

My Dad's father, Innocenzo, came to America as a young man. He died before I had a chance to know him. His wife, Lucia, lived with us for many years. She was not a very nice person and will get no mention here.

My Mom's parents were Pasquale and Caterina Camardi. They came to America as immigrants in 1912 from a little town called Grassano in Italy. They came, not expecting help from the government, but just a chance to make a life for their families. Pasquale opened a store on Rockaway Avenue where he cleaned and blocked men's hats (in the snazzy fedora days) and also had a few shoeshine stalls. Grandpa Camardi ruled over that establishment in his grey cardigan sweater and smoking a DiNoboli cigar. He worked hard and after a time was able to purchase a house on Hull Street in Brooklyn where our family spent many happy holidays.

Caterina Camardi, who worked as a seamstress after coming to America in 1912 at age 31. Her employee I.D. badge is shown in the photos. I'm guessing this picture was taken in the early 1930's. Grandma was a sweetheart, but a tough cookie too. She did all the carpentry, electrical and plumbing work around their Brooklyn house because Grandpa Pasquale was busy running his hat blocking/shoeshine store. She is the face of first-generation immigrants who helped build this country.

We recently visited Ellis Island, where so many immigrants passed through in the late 1800s and early 1900s. If you have not yet been there, especially if you had ancestors who passed through that gateway, you need to go. I was able to research the Ellis Island data base and found immigration records of my family's arrival in this country. The records tell on what ship they arrived (my grandparents came on the Brasile out of Naples) and allow you to view the ship's manifest pages to learn when and from where they departed, with whom they travelled, and what they had in their possession.

While on a walking tour of Ellis Island, we wandered into a room that displayed posters of some of the great ships that travelled in and out of that island. One poster stopped me in my tracks...it was an image of the ship "Brasile", (see photo) the very same boat that brought my grandparents to America! I felt chills all over, as if Grandpa and Grandma were sending me a little message from beyond.

It was an emotional experience for me walking those corridors and later watching a film on what the immigrant experience was like. I am so proud of my grandparents for having the courage to leave behind all that was familiar to them, and trying to create a better future for their families. I want my children to know of the sacrifices that were made by their immigrant ancestors so that they could have the privilege of living in America. The values that make them who they are were handed down by those who came before.

Pasquale and Caterina Camardi

Grandma's I.D. badge

Chapter 12: STOOP SITTING

In Brooklyn during the 1950s, our community center was the stoop. For those not familiar with the term, a "stoop" is simply a set of steps leading up to a residential entrance....whether it was just a few steps or a full flight. According to the American Heritage Dictionary, "stoop" is derived from a Dutch word (stoep) meaning "front porch." The word came to America through New Amsterdam and the Hudson Valley, and has spread from there, most commonly used in the Northeast United States. (There, now you know...one more thing you can stop wondering about.)

The stoop was a place where people from the neighborhood congregated to socialize. I wish I could tack on the time we spent on those steps to the end of my life, I would edge out Methuselah!) The stoop was home to young and old alike; every block had an old man who minded every body's business... they called him "The Mayor". Invariably, the Mayor ruled his kingdom from his lofty perch atop a stoop. Some important things to look for when selecting the best stoops:

1) Location, location, location. One reason for sitting on the stoop was to see the comings and goings in the neighborhood. This required a stoop with a lot of pedestrian traffic, preferably one near an intersection where you could see the main street and the cross street. A bus or subway stop in the vicinity was a plus because you saw people returning from work or school. A real bonus was if your stoop was near food stores; in Italian neighborhoods, Salumerias (Italian delis), bakeries and fruit stores were veritable bee hives of activity.

2) Construction. Some stoops were unsuitable vantage places. Higher stoops were better than lower ones simply because you could see more. Also, some had landings at the top of the stoop with nice, flat brick railings that were perfect for sitting; these were the "box seats" in stoopville, and very hard to come by. Because of their comfort, they were popular spots on a summer evening where people would sit waiting for the Bungalow Bar Ice Cream truck to come by after dinner. A well-built stoop was also perfect for *stoop-ball*, a game played with a Spaldeen.

3) Owner tolerance. I like the joke about an Italian's idea of a vacation....sitting on someone else's stoop. That's exactly what we did. Well-constructed stoops in good locations were not enough; you also required a home owner who would tolerate groups of teens lounging on their stoop every day for hours on end. If you were lucky, one of your friends lived in such a house, making it less likely (but not a sure thing) that the home owner wouldn't chase you away. Most parents were happy to know their kid was sitting just outside the door, and would cut you some slack if you cleaned up your soda bottles and cigarette butts.

As people walked by the stoop, there would be exchanges with the stoop sitters. "Hey moron, your Yankees lost today, this is the Dodgers year." The reply: "How many World Series the Dodgers been to, pinhead." Or: "Hey Sal, when you gonna pay me the two bucks I loaned you?" The reply: "What are you, the Dime Savings Bank? I'll pay you Sunday." Of course there was a lot of girl watching going on too. Those were the days when girls walked around in pairs, wearing tight pedal-pusher pants, satin jackets, tight sweaters with those Madonna "bullet bras" underneath, and of course the obligatory kerchief covering up rows and rows of hair curlers.

In Brooklyn, in the wonderful 1950s when the world was young, "The Stoop" was our vantage point on the world. Now we sit in Starbucks.

Teenaged me in front of our old stoop

Chapter 11: AT THE "LIBERRY"

I was a secret reader as a kid. Starting probably around fourth grade, I began a lifelong love of books. Histories, biographies, fiction…anything I could get my hands on helped me experience the world in my little corner of Brooklyn. I say "secret reader" because in my old neighborhood, we didn't sit around on the stoop discussing the latest books we had read. Your standing on the block was not at all improved if you were considered a "bookworm". In spite of my suspicious trips to the Saratoga Avenue branch "Liberry" as we called it, I passed street muster because I was good at sports, street games, and almost never turned down a "double-dog dare".

Anyhow, back to the "liberry". The interior was dark and dusty, and the place smelled of books, a wonderful smell by the way. It was filled with tables where kids could read or do homework. It was also a place where old folks could come in from the cold and warm up for a bit. The walls were covered with card catalog files where the titles, authors and shelf locations were methodically listed, thanks to the wonder of the Dewey Decimal System. When you borrowed a book, the librarian rubber-stamped the due date for its return on a card in the back of the book. Every kid my age knew where all the *forbidden* books were like "Peyton Place" and "Lady Chatterley's Lover" ; if you held them in your hand, they practically fell open to the well-thumbed pages with the "hot" parts!

In the Fifties, librarians were a strict lot. They were expert "shushers" and tolerated little guff from kids. This was way back when children still had some respect for authority figures, so we actually obeyed them! They could also be helpful and even *solicitous* when they found a little barbarian among us who shared their love of books. Our librarian at the Saratoga branch would set aside books she thought you would like, and slip them to you rather than put them back into general circulation. Thanks to that kind lady, I got to read some good books I probably would not have picked myself. Yes it's true, I was a twelve-year old library gigolo.

Things have changed since I was a kid. Although "bookworms" are still not high up on the kiddy pecking order, they are better tolerated and less likely to be beat up. Reading materials are more available than they used to be, what with books being electronically down loadable from the library, books on audio CDs, and more branch libraries in existence than ever before. Ironically, computers have also created the greatest competition to reading as a pastime, with the rise of the hated video games to which kids are so addicted.

Parents listen up...don't deprive your children of the gift of reading. Switch off the damn X-box and give them some reading time; they will thank you for it down the road.

Chapter 12: BAND-AID PARK

Parents are so overprotective of their kids these days. They would *shudder* if they ever visited the playgrounds of my youth. It's not that our parents didn't worry about us, they just had to make do with the places available for kids to play. Our most frequented playground was in Callahan & Kelly Park, which lies at the northern edge of the Brooklyn neighborhood of Brownsville on Truxton Street, beneath the elevated "Broadway Line" subway. (For the record, "elevated subway" is an oxymoron.)

The park was large for a neighborhood playground, with baseball diamonds, basketball, handball and bocce courts, horseshoe throwing pits, picnic tables and of course the children's playground. Also, the park was lit at night, which made it great for summer evening activities. The playgrounds of today are designed and built to be "child-safe". The play areas are constructed of plastic with no sharp edges; hand rails are on every raised platform; even the floor is rubberized in case, heaven forbid, a child should fall down.

The Callahan & Kelly playground was a minefield of dangerous activities. Everything was made of steel that heated up in the mid-day sun; wood filled with skin-piercing splinters, and unforgiving concrete floors that did not treat kiddy knees and skulls kindly. The typical things to play on in every Brooklyn playground included swings, slides (called sliding ponds), see-saws and of course every parent's favorite, the dreaded monkey bars. There was also a wading pool, basically a concrete enclosure surrounded by steel bars, that was flooded by a series of sprinkler heads that surrounded the pool.

The swings were of two types, "kiddy" and what we called "the big swings". Except for being made of stainless steel, which on a hot day could nicely broil a small child in about five minutes, the kiddy swings were relatively safe. The big swings were another matter. Typically, one did not sit on them as intended, but rather stood up and pumped one's little legs to propel the swing higher and higher. There was no limit to how high the swings could go, and in the process of trying to impress one's friends, kids were known to fly well *above* the horizontal bar from which the swings were suspended.

Besides being able to make pancakes on its surface on a hot day, the slide featured other hazards. If the slide got sticky, say from someone spilling a Coke on it, the kid would slide a few feet, stick on the tacky surface, and tumble down the rest of the way, or worse, off the edge of the slide onto the friendly concrete floor. Climbing *up* the slide instead of using the ladder also resulted in frequent "owies" and souvenir band aids.

The see-saw seems harmless enough. One child sits on either end and laughingly enjoys going up and down. Not in our playground. One fun prank was to quickly push down on your end just as the other kid was straddling his end to get on. This contributed to the steady flow of boys entering the priesthood in my neighborhood. It also kept our local dentists supplied with orthodontia work. Another gag was to first lower your end all the way, which naturally elevated the other kid as high as he could go. And then suddenly jumping off your side and watching the kid on the other end come crashing down onto, you guessed it, the concrete floor. It is thought that the term "pain in the ass" originated from this practice.

And now, the king of kiddie playground injuries, *the monkey bars*. In ancient Egypt, Pharaoh sought to eliminate the Israelites by killing all their first-born sons. If only he had known about the monkey bars. The designer of this apparatus must have been horribly teased as a boy, and his vengeance was well wrought upon the sons of his tormentors. A pyramid-like structure about twenty feet high, built of steel pipes made to be climbed or swung from. Again, if used carefully, the monkey bars were safe enough. A rite of passage in our group, however, was to climb to the uppermost bars and *stand on the top bars* without holding on to anything. There are definitely kids walking around today who can't do long-division because their attempts to accomplish this feat failed miserably.

As for the wading pool, other than falling on the concrete floor, or getting hung up climbing the pointed, wrought iron fence, this was a relatively low risk activity. Of course if the park attendant or "parkie" as we called him didn't thoroughly sweep out the broken beer bottles from the night before, there could be stitches in your future, but on a hot day, we were prepared to take our chances. Kids in their bathing suits enjoyed sitting on the gushing sprinkler heads. If you haven't done this, it's hard to understand the feeling. It's why, even as adults in the Jacuzzi we gravitate to the inlet water jets just to recreate that thrill.

Disneyworld and $5,000 vacations were off in the future. All we had were wood and steel and concrete, and we sure as hell made the most of them.

Me on the monkey bars with cousin Millie

Chapter 13: LOUIE'S CANDY STORE

In the 1950s, the candy store was an integral part of every Brooklyn neighborhood. We had several, but Louie's under the el on Fulton Street was our regular hangout. Louie and his wife Miriam ran the place with help from a dark, pretty woman named Flo on whom I had a huge crush, and their son Howard who sometimes worked weekends. There was a news stand out front where you could pick up a 5 cent copy of the Daily News or Mirror. Inside was a soda fountain with half a dozen stools, a counter covered with candy and a whole wall covered with comic books. Higher up that wall out of a kid's reach were the girlie magazines that Louie didn't want us drooling over.

As we got older we spent time there almost every night. In back of the store was a red ice chest filled with frosty-cold sodas and baseball game machine that we pumped our hard-earned dimes into trying to break the high score. We sat at the counter for an egg cream or Lime Rickey to enjoy the view as Flo bent over to hand pack pints of Dolly Madison Ice Cream. Also such specialty items as Mello-Rolls (a cylinder-shaped ice cream you put in a specially shaped cone, and even Dixie Cups, small containers of ice cream with pictures of celebrities in the lids. We traded these among ourselves.

There were also two old-fashioned wooden phone booths in the back with the phone directories chained to the side. Local bookies shuttled back and forth between Louie's and the Sportsman Café across the street to ply their trade. Louie tolerated them because I think he liked getting a bet down on the sly when Miriam wasn't looking.

One day, beaming with pride Louie told us their son Howard had graduated from medical school and become a doctor. I wonder how many egg creams and comic books Louie and Miriam had to sell to pay for that. We never saw Howard much after he became Dr. Howard. I guess it would be unseemly for a doctor to be making malteds at the counter in a candy store. I went into the Army in 1960, but I believe the candy store was still there when I left, minus one part-time helper. Louie and Miriam's story is the same as other children of immigrants; sacrifice for the children's education. My father worked two jobs as long as I can remember. For her entire life my mother always put herself last.

Their sacrifice helped my generation better ourselves, but it also contributed to our moving away from the old neighborhoods we now remember so fondly. 1950s Brooklyn is gone. It was a special place in a bygone time and I feel privileged to have been a part of it.

Chapter 14:   UNCLE JIM

Whoever coined the phrase "strong, silent type" must have known my Uncle Jim. His given name was Innocenzo, and according to immigration records, he arrived from Grassano, Italy in 1921 on the ship Canada. He married my mother's sister Anna and lived in a house down the block from us in Brooklyn. Uncle Jim spoke broken English his whole life. He was too busy working construction and supporting his wife and four children to ever find the time to polish his language skills. Like many first-generation Italian immigrants, he made his living with his hands.

Uncle Jim never said much but he had a smile that lit up his weathered, sunburned face. He had a full head of jet black hair with iron grey streaks that he combed straight back. If you brushed against him, you could feel the muscles under his shirt, the result of a lifetime of physical labor. He never said much at family dinners, but his intelligent eyes followed the conversation of laughter, teasing and arguing that was typical around our family table. He had a habit that fascinated me…he would take out a pen knife and carefully slice slivers of a long Italian hot pepper, seeds and all, onto his plate of pasta.

Most of the men in our neighborhood were blue-collar guys. I would see them heading to the subway in their work clothes carrying lunch pails with them and maybe a copy of the Daily News or Il Progresso, the Italian newspaper, under their arms. Back in the early days of America, men like these built our cities…skyscrapers, bridges, roads and subways. Many, like Uncle Jim, were Italian. They worked cheap and they worked hard so that maybe their children wouldn't have to rely on strong backs to make a living. They accomplished much and endured much, all for "la famiglia".

It shames me to admit that many of us, with our college educations and white collar jobs, felt superior to them back then. How wrong we were. They came to a new country, did work no one else wanted, and established a tradition of respect for education and a work ethic on which their descendants would build. I know they would be proud of what their children and grandchildren achieved. In their modesty, they would view us as so much better than them, but in reality, we aren't worthy to carry their lunch pails.

To my Uncle Jim and all first-generation immigrants: I salute you.

My Uncle Jim (James Lagonigro)

Chapter 15: FESTA ITALIANA

My boyhood parish church, Our Lady of Lourdes held a carnival every year to raise money. It was a schoolyard affair with the usual kiddie rides, and *rigged* games of chance (wink, wink) under canvass tents. It was OK, but not nearly as much fun as the authentic Italian street feast held annually in the parish where I was baptized, Our Lady of Loreto. Pacific Street was closed to traffic from Sackman Street near the church entrance to Eastern Parkway, a main area thoroughfare that led to the Brooklyn Museum, the Brooklyn Botanical Gardens, and the upscale neighborhood of Park Slope where my lovely wife was raised.

The street feast was an Italian tradition that immigrants to America recreated as a way to remember "the old country." Throughout Italy, street feasts were common in every town, usually sponsored by the church, most likely as a celebration commemorating the patron saint of the village. It is the very essence of what it means to be Italian. Our Lady of Loreto was predominantly an Italian parish with at least one Sunday Mass always said in that language. It was only natural for these good people to cling to their heritage by staging these feasts or "festas". They may have passed their American citizenship tests, and couldn't be prouder of their new country, but underneath, in their heart of hearts, they would always be Italians.

The feast lasted about 3-4 days...usually Thursday through Sunday. The excitement in the neighborhood was high, after all, this was the poor kids' Disneyworld. There were truck-mounted rides like the Whip, the Ferris Wheel and the Moon Swing. They had games of chance like the spinning wheels where you put your dime on a number hoping to win that shiny new toaster for Mom, or trying to toss a small wooden ring onto the glass neck a Coke bottle, and of course the rows and rows of fish bowls filled with colored water into which you tossed ping-pong balls. If you won, you got to keep the goldfish, which had a life expectancy of about 15 minutes after you got it home. It then got flushed, or as we referred to it, "burial at sea!"

That there was food goes without saying; this was an *Italian* feast! The next time someone invents a new appetite suppressant pill, I have a sure-fire way of testing it. Let the test subject take the new pill. Then bring him to an outdoor Italian feast and find a stand where sausages and peppers are cooking on the grill. Make sure the sausages have been cooking for at least an hour, and are just starting to caramelize. Position the test subject downwind from the stand for five minutes. If he can resist begging the owner of the stand to sell him a sandwich at any price, then the pill may be considered effective. Most people will cave, as you can readily see in Exhibit A above.

For dessert after your sausage and pepper hero, you must have some Zeppolis…dough fried in very hot oil, placed in a paper bag and sprinkled with powdered sugar. You shake the bag to coat the hot Zeppolis with sugar, and then shove one into your face. If you don't get some powdered sugar on the tip of your nose, you're not eating them properly. Don't have your cholesterol count taken within 24 hours of eating one.) The other kind of Zeppoli is the type served at the feast, basically,

The feast also featured music, the kind of Italian songs that can be played on simple instruments by old men wearing grey cardigan sweaters with a DiNoboli cigar stub in the pocket. If there was some extra money in the budget, the church would erect a makeshift bandstand that would give any OSHA Inspector palpitations. Sometimes they marched while they played, usually leading the women's Rosary Sodality in the procession carrying the statue of the church's patron saint. Pinned to the statue was *money*… ones, fives, tens or twenties. Once in a while you would see a rare *fifty dollar bill*, probably pinned there by a repentant sinner.

As corny as it may sound, these old songs, played and sung with real feeling, had a haunting effect on me, as if something was reaching through the centuries and pulling me back to the land of my ancestors.

Chapter 16: CONEY ISLAND MEMORIES

One of my fondest memories of childhood was a trip to the beach. If you were from Brooklyn, Coney Island or Brighton Beach were the seaside destinations of choice since they were accessible by train. Rockaway Beach in Queens was also an option, but traveling there from Brooklyn by public transportation involved visas and passing through customs. Besides, Queens was a strange, exotic borough where they had trees and other suspicious things. Even to get to Coney we had to take two trains, the "A" train from our Rockaway Avenue Station to Franklin Avenue, and then upstairs to the elevated Franklin shuttle all the way to the end of the line. At the time, this train had straw-covered seats, something that could never last with today's vandalism-prone riders.

As you approached Coney Island, you smelled the ocean through the open train windows. Then the fabulous parachute jump loomed in the background and hooray, you were there. As your mother dragged you by the hand for the short walk to the beach, the sights, sounds and smells overwhelmed you. Coney Island along the boardwalk and streets was a riot of rides, snack stands, freak shows and carnival games. The original Nathan's sold hot dogs that had a juicy *snap* when you bit into them, crispy, crinkle-cut French fries in a paper cup, and the unlikely but delicious treat, chow-mein on a bun. Nathan's is still there, and despite years of decline, Coney Island is on the rise again.

Getting from the boardwalk to the spot on the beach where you wanted to set up your blanket involved a Brooklyn maneuver I call the "Blanket Walk". The sand was burning hot, so you tried to surreptitiously step on the blankets and towels of the people you passed along the way. I can remember the poor ice cream guy who walked around all day in the hot sand carrying a box of dry ice and hollering: "Get Your Good Humor and "Humorettes". We always brought lunch and a jug full of Kool Aid to save money. If they ever found one of those old brown bags soaked in oil from our pepper and egg sandwiches, they would have to call out a Hazmat team for disposal.

Late afternoon at the beach was a nice time for things like looking for seashells and making sand castles. The crowds thinned out and sometimes you got to sit in the lifeguard's chair. Usually around 5 pm we would head up to the boardwalk for a visit to Steeplechase Park (see 10/6/08 post). Steeplechase was a fabulous place that sadly is gone today, but anybody who was lucky enough to visit will never forget such rides in and around the park as the Steeplechase Horses, the Panama Slide, the Parachute Jump, the Wonder Wheel and of course, one of America's last great wooden roller coasters, the Cyclone.

This was also our time to get the great soft custard they dispensed from machines on the boardwalk in vanilla, chocolate, or my favorites, pistachio and banana.

The train trip home was a long one, with a damp bathing suit, sand in your sneakers and a sun burn that would have to be dealt with in the morning. But it was all worth it...Coney Island is a place out of our carefree youth, and when we think back to the good times we had there, (in spite of the medicine bottles lined up on the counter), we are young again if only for a little while.

Chapter 17:   THE DENTIST FROM HELL

Remember that scary scene from the movie "Marathon Man" when bad guy Sir Laurence Oliver was torturing poor Dustin Hoffman with a dentist's drill to get him to talk? If I check the credits I'll bet my old dentist, Dr. Martinelli, was the technical advisor for that scene. Dr. Martinelli had an office on Fulton Street, just off Rockaway Avenue in the old neighborhood. I think he leased that space because the sounds of the elevated train that passed just outside his window drowned out the screams coming from his office.

The office was in one of those typical Brooklyn apartment buildings with mostly residential units with some commercial space for offices and stores on the ground floor. As I recall, the doctor's office was on the second floor, reached by stairs from the lobby. The lobby was no more than a landing where the building super kept his kids' bikes chained to the garbage pails under the stairs. When the building was constructed, they somehow permanently infused the lobby with the smell of cooking cabbage that I'm sure lingers there to this day.

As you entered the office, the first thing you saw against the wall was a stainless-steel, glass-doored cabinet filled with an assortment of dental instruments developed during the Spanish Inquisition. Sharp picks, tiny hammers, pliers, clamps and other scary paraphernalia that immediately struck terror into the heart of a small child. Why Dr. Martinelli chose this cabinet of horrors to be the first thing patients were confronted with, I'll never know. Perhaps it was to send a message: "This ain't gonna be a day at the beach, little man."

Usually the person who greeted you was Tessie, the doctor's receptionist/nurse/office assistant. If they ever made a movie of Dr. Martinelli's life, Tessie would be played by Shelly Winters. She was a classically tough Brooklyn blonde. Under that gruff exterior was an even gruffer interior. Tessie took no lip, either from the patients or her boss. She and the doctor communicated by screaming at each other. They were an odd couple to be sure, with mutual animosity being the only thing they had in common.

Dr. Martinelli was a strikingly handsome man, tall and slim, with a full head of black hair streaked with silver. Unfortunately, his benevolent appearance belied his satanic nature. First of all, he used novocaine only in cases of imminent death. The drill he used was a massive piece of porcelain and metal machinery complete with whirring motors and leather belts. For all this firepower, the freakin' drill made about six revolutions a minute...you could actually count them! And to add to the fun, smoke came out of your mouth because the low drill speed created friction on the tooth's unyielding surface!

Once the hole had been drilled in the tooth, Dr. Death (without benefit of Novocaine remember) would bring out the ultimate pain-producing instrument, the air hose that blew pressurized cold air into the sensitive cavity. That would have got Dustin Hoffman to talk! Oh, I forgot to mention, the whole time he was working on you, it was not uncommon for Dr. Martinelli to have a cigarette in his mouth with the ash dangling precariously over your gaping maw.

In the days before fluoride, cavities were far more common than today. Most folks my age have a mouth full of silver, and the psychological scars to prove they paid the price for their cavities.

Chapter 18:   MISS FRANKIE

She was in her mid-thirties with powdered skin, cotton-candy blond hair worn like Barbara Stanwick's in "Double Indemnity", and pouty red lips. She wore flowered dresses, tinted eye glasses and always smelled so nice. She was Miss Frankie, our grammar school art teacher. During the 1950s at Our Lady of Lourdes school, Miss Frankie did her best to light the fire of artistic passion in a collection of rag-tag kids from the streets of Brooklyn. Each child paid the princely sum of 21 cents a week to cover the salaries of Miss Frankie, and our far less glamorous music teacher, Miss Hessian. The fee also helped pay for afternoon movies every Monday shown in the church basement...such classics as "Francis the Talking Mule" with Donald O'Connor, and the adventure serial "The Thunder Riders" with cowboy Gene Autry.

As I recall we had art class on Tuesdays. Miss Frankie would breeze in with an armful of rolled-up paper that she would tack up and proceed to show us, step-by-step, how to draw a vase full of flowers or some other innocuous still life. She would begin the drawing, and then wander around the room to see how her pupils were progressing. Miss Frankie was not overly tolerant of deviations in style or technique; she wanted you to copy what she had drawn, *exactly* as she had drawn it. She would correct your drawing to make it look like hers, thus stifling any ideas of artistic interpretation. Picasso or Monet would have grown up to become plumbers if they had Miss Frankie as their first art teacher.

I could always draw pretty well, and easily reproduced the line drawing for the day in the style approved by Miss Frankie. Because of this she would usually glide by my desk and simply nod, saying: "Very good James" before moving on to the next student. When she didn't like what she saw, Miss Frankie would bend down over the drawing, her lovely scent filling the air, and proceed to modify the offending artist's rendition so it looked more like hers. I was in love with Miss Frankie, and wanted so much for her face to be near mine as she corrected my work. Because of this, I was not above setting aside my artistic integrity and intentionally tanking a drawing just to get the benefit of Miss Frankie's suggestions.

Art class was a welcome break for our regular teachers since they got a brief respite from the 45 or so kids they were charged with enlightening each day. That may sound like a lot compared to today's classes of 20-25, but remember, this was a Catholic school where discipline was king. Unruly children were never a problem for long. One trip to the Principal's office where Brother Justinian awaited (Darth Vader was modeled after him) was usually enough to take the starch out of any kid who put a toe over the line. As a result, teachers could concentrate on teaching, and the results bore out the effort required to maintain decorum in the classroom.

We all wore school uniforms so there were no fashionistas to set themselves above other kids. Your hygiene was always subject to inspection, and there was no reluctance to send notes home suggesting more frequent shampoos or finger nail cleaning. During a class, if the Principal or any other teacher entered the room, we would all stand and say in unison: "Good morning Brother Justinian." Kids so respected teachers that we stood in the rain fighting to carry a teachers books or shield them with our umbrellas. We tried hard to get picked for menial jobs like washing the blackboards or packing textbooks away at the end of the school year. Older boys were*allowed* to go grocery shopping in Bohack's for the food used by the brothers and nuns who lived on the church grounds.

But I digress...back to my muse, Miss Frankie. I never knew whether "Frankie" was her first or last name, but despite the rather narrow artistic boundaries she set, I owe her a debt for instilling in me an interest in art. This was nurtured by a Brooklyn Tech high school teacher, whose name is gone from my memory. This woman encouraged me to try for a career in commercial art, but unfortunately my days at Brooklyn Tech came to an end soon after some bad decisions I made caused me and the school to part company.

Teaching should be one of the noblest professions anyone can choose because of the potential to influence and shape young lives. Sadly, the bureaucrats have turned teachers into civil servants, thereby severely limiting their ability to inspire. To all the teachers who rise above the system and give their all every day, we should say thank you. "A good teacher is like a candle - it consumes itself to light the way for others." ~Author Unknown

Chapter 19: BENNY THE BARBER

You probably remember when those red, white and blue spinning poles outside a storefront meant the establishment was a barber shop, in my old Brooklyn neighborhood it meant much more. The barber shop was a gathering place where men went, not only for a haircut or a shave, but to socialize with their paisani. There were two barber shops on Rockaway Avenue, Pete's off Fulton Street, and Benny's, one block down near Hull Street. I usually went to Benny's, mainly because he had a stack of comics that kids could read while waiting. If Benny was preoccupied, a curious boy could sneak a peek at the risqué Esquire magazines. If Benny caught you it meant a smack on the back of the head.

On the long mirrored counter was a tall glass container filled with blue fluid and combs being disinfected. There was also a line of bottles containing hair creams and shaving lotions like Wildroot Crème Oil and Vitalis. I was intrigued by the little machine that produced hot shaving lather at the touch of a button. These were places patronized mostly by Italian men whose main hobby, after eating of course, was arguing. Out of the blue, one would make a pronouncement, like a Senator on the floor of Congress, and someone else would immediately take up the challenge. Before long, the words were flying along with the hair...hands adorned with pinky rings gestured wildly in the air. I learned how to curse in fluent Italian in Benny's chair.

Pete's was owned by my friend Johnny's father. Rumor had it that a sporting man could lay down a bet at Pete's with one of the bookies who hung out there under the hot towels. On any given day, especially around Christmas, you could also buy deeply discounted merchandise that "fell off the truck". For 75 cents, you got the same haircut everybody else got, finished off with some of that nice hot lather to shave the back of your neck, and a dusting of talcum powder. You walked out feeling like a new man. Now men pay crazy prices to go to 'salons' for haircuts; sadly, the barber poles are mostly gone along with the camaraderie to be found there.

Shops like Benny's and Pete's, and dozens of other small stores, were part of real neighborhoods where people knew each other and had your back. It's different now... people live in the suburbs with nice lawns, and the big box stores have replaced the Mom and Pop operations. They're nice places to live, but they don't fit my definition of neighborhoods.

Chapter 20: THE POWER OF FORMICA

I look at the appliances and gadgets around my house and think about the days when things were much simpler. No exotic coffee makers, (no exotic coffees for that matter), no air conditioning, computers, cell phones, video games, microwaves, none of the things we take for granted in modern life. But we were happy with what we had. I read an article recently about how the 2003 blackout in New York City actually brought families and neighborhoods together because all of the electronic distractions that take up our attention were not available. People actually spoke to each other.

Take the kitchen for example. Now there are all kinds of streamlined kitchen counter configurations with stools and easy-to-make instant meals designed for the convenience of varying family schedules and food preferences. Growing up, I sat with my parents, sister and brother at the Formica and chrome table in the kitchen. We ate the home-cooked meal Mom had made and talked about what went on during our day. I find it funny that psychologists now recommend sitting at the table for family dinners as a way to promote togetherness and quality family time. We did the same thing, but we called it eating.

After dinner we would listen to the radio, or when we finally got one, watch our favorite shows on the RCA black and white TV. I remember feeling happy hearing my mother laugh out loud at the Jack Benny or Red Skeleton Shows. I would watch the Yankee games with my father and talk a little baseball. One of my jobs was to keep him supplied with cold Piels beers. We were apart during the day, what with work and school, and this was our time to be together as a family. I even took a time out from teasing my sister when we watched kiddy shows like Howdy Doody and The Mickey Mouse Club together. Music was played on a multi-speed "Victrola", a turntable that spun 78 rpm vinyl records, and had an adaptor for playing 45 rpms when they came out. No I-pods, no down loads, but it was good enough.

Our refrigerator was a Kelvinator with old-fashioned ice cube trays. No automatic ice maker, no instant cold water, just a box with a tiny freezer that had to be manually defrosted. We survived. For many years my mother did laundry in a wash tub, and hung it out to dry on a clothes line. When we got a washing machine it was a big deal. We never did get a dryer. Somehow, Mom managed. We actually had a toaster with little doors that opened on either side. You placed the bread in, closed the doors, and a heating element toasted the bread. You had to watch it because there was no timer or darkness setting. Smoke billowing out of the toaster meant you had waited too long. Know what...it made better toast than the damn fancy toaster I have now.

Frozen foods were just making their appearance, so everything we ate was fresh from the grocery store. No propane grill in the back yard...we barbecued using charcoal briquettes and lighter fluid. It wasn't uncommon to see men without eyebrows in the summer. In the days before microwaves, I remember what a splash TV dinners made when Swanson introduced them in 1953. They were a convenience to be sure, but it was the beginning of the end for sit-down family dinners at the kitchen table. Now everybody sat in front of the TV eating off folding trays. One small luxury we had must have been a wedding gift to my parents because we couldn't afford to buy it. It was a Westinghouse electric sandwich press that made the best damn grilled cheese sandwiches I ever ate.

Funny but it seems like the more modern conveniences that got introduced to our lives, the more isolated we became. Dads heat something up in the microwave when they get home late from work. Kids bring dinner to their rooms so they don't have to be away from Facebook for a whole hour. Mom pops in a Lean Cuisine before heading off to Pilates. Is it possible that a lot of the problems that lead to divorces and broken families could be solved with a Formica table?

Chapter 21:   OUR SUMMER HOME IN THE COUNTRY

Not that I was ever to made to feel that way, quite the opposite in fact, but in reality, I grew up *poor*. I always had enough to eat and clothes on my back, thanks largely to my mother's talent for squeezing ten cents out of a nickel, but there wasn't much left for anything else, like vacations. I smile when I hear kids today complaining about having to go back to Disneyworld again. "We were just there last year" they whine. "Can't we go someplace else?"

I never went on vacation *anywhere* as a kid. I don't say this for pity, it's just the way things were, and I accepted it. Most of my friends were in the same boat, so I really didn't have anybody to envy. Besides, we were too busy having "poor kid" fun. Not a day went by that I didn't wake up looking forward to playing some dopey, made-up game like those I've discussed in other posts (10/11/08, 10/14/08, 11/7/08.) I've used this line before, but it's worth repeating here: "An Italian's idea of a vacation is to sit on someone else's stoop."

We did have our "country home" in the summer. Before you get excited for me, a word of explanation. My Uncle Jim and Aunt Anna Lagonigro had what we called "the bungalow" on Elderts Lane in Brooklyn. The area at the time, down toward the Belt Parkway service road, was largely undeveloped except for a scattering of smaller homes, many without sewers or indoor plumbing. It was called "the hole". The roads were poor, and it didn't take much imagination to believe you were in some small town in the deep South. This was our *country home*, and we spent many happy weekends there with the Lagonigros, the Bivonas and my family.

The property and house were very rustic, and not at all large, but for us kids it was paradise. The house had a primitive kitchen, but it didn't stop the three sisters (my mother and two aunts) from somehow turning out the most fantastic Italian dinners, which we ate outdoors at a wooden table shaded by a grapevine. The beer and homemade wine were always plentiful, and after dinner, while the adults talked, played cards and relaxed, the kids had the run of the place. There were blackberry bushes on the grounds and we ate the fruit right off the bushes. There was also an old cherry tree that shaded the house, and the cherries were delicious.

There was no television to park ourselves in front of, no Game Boy or X-Box, I'm not sure the property even had *electricity*. That meant we had to devise amusements for ourselves, something today's kids almost never get to do. The cousins would play checkers, have a catch, jump rope, maybe a game of hide-and-go-seek....simple pleasures that we thoroughly enjoyed. There were trees to climb, comics to read, tin cans to throw rocks at, and woodsy corners of the property to explore. Cousins of all ages, boys and girls, played together until it was time to eat or go home.

There was a well and water pump at the bungalow that I loved using, and a spider-filled outhouse that no matter how much lime was thrown down that hole, you always knew *exactly* where you were. We got to walk freely around the neighborhood (if you could call it that) since there was almost no traffic on the dirt roads. There was what can only be described as a "general store" around the corner that sold a little bit of everything. I remember a favorite purchase was the paper kites they sold, all rolled up, that had to be assembled before flying. We also bought two rolls of kite string that we tied together so that the kite could be flown higher. Negotiating the overhead electric cables required skill, but being city kids, we managed just fine.

These were our "vacations" in the fifties, no frills to be sure. Maybe it's the phenomenon that makes things from the past always seem better when remembered many years later, but those weekend trips to the bungalow, to this day, have a special place in my heart. Spending time with people you loved and who loved you, and gladly sharing whatever you had, is an experience that can't be easily put into words. We may have been "*poor*", but no amount of money could buy the togetherness and good times we shared.

I have since been to many places on vacation, and I always have a good time. If you asked me if I would ever trade a modern-day vacation with all the trimmings for a weekend at Aunt Anna's bungalow, my answer would probably surprise you.

Chapter 22: ANGELO AND TESSIE

As a kid I realized things at home were tight, so I always tried to hustle a buck. For an eighth grader with no experience, jobs were hard to come by. I would shovel snow or run errands for people in the neighborhood for nickels and dimes. My Aunt Mary and Uncle Nick had a small dressmaking business on Jamaica Avenue in Brooklyn. Diagonally across the street stood a store that sold fruit, cold cuts, bread, beer and soda, and a few household necessities. I guess it would be called a deli today, but in the Fifties we just referred to it by the name of the owner, as in "Go to Angelo's and get me a container of milk."

Thanks to a recommendation from Aunt Mary, I started working at Angelo's after school and on weekends. Angelo was an older man who never wore anything but pizza-man undershirts and dirty khakis covered by an equally dirty apron. He had a perpetually sad, basset hound expression on his face, but the gentlest disposition of anyone I ever met. Angelo's wife had passed away in childbirth, and the child she delivered, Tessie, helped her father run the store. I guess as Angelo got older, lugging heavy beer and soda cases up and down the stairs became too much for him. Also, he wanted to compete with another neighborhood store who began delivering groceries to homes in the area.

I rode my bike to work since it was too far to walk from my house. I used a big wagon to deliver the orders that Angelo would pack into brown bags. The amount of the order was written on the side of one of the bags, and Angelo would give me some singles and loose coins in case I had to make change. The area I delivered in was a cut above where I lived, and most people would throw me a quarter for the delivery. Once I pushed a loaded wagon up the steep hill that was Miller Avenue and delivered to an older woman living on one of the poshest streets in Brooklyn, Highland Avenue. She gave me what I thought was a dollar tip and I shoved it into my pocket. When I got back to the store, I pulled it out and it was a ten! I thought about going back to ask her if she made a mistake, but then I thought about where she lived and where I lived, and the ten stayed in my pocket.

When Tessie got to know me, she would sit me down on the bench outside the store and just talk. She was a large, rather homely looking girl of maybe 25, and she seemed lonely. She would ask about my family and friends, what I liked to do, did I date girls, and who my favorite movie stars were. I didn't think much of it at the time, after all, chatting with Tessie was a lot easier on a hot day than shlepping cases of beer and soda down to the cellar. Angelo rarely bothered us during these little chats. I sensed he knew Tessie was lonely, and that somehow these talks with me eased things a bit. Angelo even softened up and let me work the cash register, something I could tell he was loath to do. It infringed on his status somehow as the store's owner and proprietor.

One thing I always wanted to do, but could never convince Angelo to give me the nod on, was to work the cold cut slicing machine. In the deli business the guy who slices the cold cuts is the top dog. Knowing how to adjust the slicer for different thicknesses of baloney, and to have those slices fall gently into your free hand while you pushed the slicer with the other is like a choreographed ballet. Angelo was a smart man and probably saw a trip to the emergency room in my future if I ever got anywhere near that machine. I would console myself with a trip to the basement where I would drink warm beer from the bottle. Angelo never let on that he missed the bottles, but I figure he just included them in my employee benefits package.

While at work I was free to eat and drink as much as I wanted. I probably ate the equivalent of my weekly salary, since I could really put it away when I was a skinny kid. Every Saturday that sweet old man would pay me in cash, and fill a bag with cold cuts and fruit for my mother. I'm sure those little extras helped us out a lot in the weeks when my father had a bad run at the race track. The Boy Scouts teach the concept of "giving back" to the community in recognition of those who may have helped us along in life.

There were so many people in my life like Angelo who had faith in me or showed me a kindness...I have tried my best to pass it forward.

Chapter 23: PENNY SERANADE

One of the small thrills of childhood was finding a penny in the street. It's hard to understand this in today's inflationary times where pocket change hardly buys anything, much less the lowly penny. Pennies are left on counters in the "take one, put one" cup as if it has become a nuisance to even carry them. I know few people who would bother to stoop down to pick one up. This certainly wasn't the case in the 1950s when I grew up. Cans were just coming into their own as containers for beer and soda, and glass bottles were still very much around. These were "kid currency" because of the deposit they could be returned for; two cents for small bottles and five cents for large. Cha-ching!

Pennies still had value in the Fifties. There were glass cases with sliding doors in the candy stores that contained 20 or 30 different candies you could buy for a penny. Mary Janes, licorice sticks, gum drops, wax lips, tiny wax bottles filled with sweet syrup, bubble gum, Tootsie Rolls, the paper strips covered with colored sugar dots, caramels, spearmint leaves and those orange, peanut-shaped marshmallows. We would stand there with a few pennies clutched in our hand trying to make a selection as if we were buying a new car, while the long-suffering store owner waited patiently to ring up his big sale.

Vending machines took pennies for gumballs, those little two-packs of Chicklets, peanuts and pistachio nuts. You could get your weight and fortune at the drugstore scale for a penny. Candy stores and delis sold "loosies" (individual cigarettes) for one penny each. You could slake your thirst at the soda fountain with a glass of "two cents plain" (seltzer). We pitched pennies against a wall to pass the time, and I remember playing penny poker after holiday dinners with my aunts, uncles and cousins. There were penny arcades where a 50 cent bankroll could get you through the afternoon.

The thing about growing up in those days, when money was always tight and pennies were precious, is that it leaves an imprint. I had a good career and we are comfortable financially, but I still look for bargains. I love breakfast and dinner specials; I can't remember the last time I made a significant purchase without waiting for it to go on sale; I confess to buying overpriced Starbucks coffee, but then I reuse the cups at home, as if to atone for my extravagance. This little "Penny Serenade" is really a tribute to the lost art of thrift.

I dislike people who are cheap. I can spend money with the best of them, as the smoke coming off my American Express card will attest, but deep inside is still a kid trying to get the most for his five-cent deposit.

Chapter 24: THE LORDS OF BOCCE

We were walking recently along the boardwalk in South Beach (not Miami, Staten Island) when we passed what looked like bocce courts. We detoured from our route and came across "The Staten Island Bocce Club". Besides three beautifully maintained bocce courts, there was a gazebo with picnic tables and a tiny garden where the members grew tomatoes and zucchini. As sometimes happens when we come upon a sight that is connected to our past, I was immediately transported in time back to Brooklyn in the 1950s where groups of old Italian men played serious bocce games on the courts in Callahan and Kelly Park on Truxton Street.

Bocce for the average player is very simple. There may be anywhere from two to four to eight players on a team. Players are awarded one point for each ball closer than the opponent's closest ball nearest to the pallino ball (the smallest ball, which has already been thrown onto the field). Each player is given two balls (boccia). A player continues to roll their balls until they get closer than the opponent's ball. Players may also throw on the fly (volo), striking the ball to move the point ball. Balls, including the pallino, may also be displaced by the balls of other players. Bocce is an inexpensive game of thought and strategy that brings families and friends together with the enjoyment of a game that everyone can play."

The men I remember played every day in Callahan-Kelly Park. They wore old pants because of the clay dust kicked up on the courts. They also wore grey cardigan sweaters and brown or grey fedora hats to complete the uniform. Most smoked smelly Di Nobili cigars which they rested on the court railing or in the band of their hat when it came their turn to throw. They always cursed in Italian and gestured wildly for every good or bad throw. If a call was close they invariably took off their belts and used them to measure. If you ever watched a game you would swear the contestants were mortal enemies, but Italians tend to be like that. After the game they would sit on the park benches together and enjoy homemade wine out of glass flasks or eat cherries they had soaked in alcohol.

Bocce is a game that can be enjoyed by anyone. On a recent family reunion picnic we had a game of bocce and it was terrific. Old guys like me played alongside 10 year old boys and we enjoyed ourselves equally. While playing with my sons and cousins, I felt a real connection to the old country.

I know my ancestors back in Grassano in Basilicata in southern Italy must have spent some time playing bocce with their families and so we were continuing a long tradition. It must have been very hard for the early immigrants to America who came here with nothing but a dream about a land that promised a better life than the one they left. They banded together with others like them who had come before, living hard lives in overcrowded neighborhoods.

I'd like to think that a game of bocce brightened some of their afternoons just as the sight of The Staten Island Bocce Club brightened mine so many years later.

Chapter 25: BARBEQUED LASAGNA

In my family, going on a picnic was no casual affair. The invasion of Normandy required less planning than an Italian family picnic. It began by deciding where to go. At first it was Alley Pond park, on the Queens border; just a short ride from Brooklyn. In later years, after some of the family moved to Long Island, it was Belmont State park in Suffolk County, an eternity away. Did they speak English in this place? Could we ever find our way home? To quote Dorothy in the Wizard of Oz: "Toto, I've got a feeling we're not in Kansas anymore".

For some reason we usually made these excursions on Sundays. In today's traffic one can learn to speak a foreign language while traveling from Brooklyn to Long Island on a Sunday, but in the Fifties, it wasn't that bad yet. There was traffic though, and to keep our caravan of cars together, we employed the "white hanky" gambit. The lead car (Uncle Nick more often than not) would tie a white handkerchief to the *"aerial"* (we never called them antennas) so that every trailing car could see the white hanky and follow, even in traffic. Of course, the white hanky was used by other caravans too, a fact that clearly diminished its effectiveness.

Once at the park, the next step was picnic table selection. Sometimes a family member would go early and try to save a group of tables, but in New York picnic grounds, where tables were scarce, this could lead to a trip to the Emergency Room. The next step was to fetch the water for the pasta. (Pasta you say, at a barbecue! Hey, we were Italian and it was Sunday. There *is* no wiggle room here.) The water would take a long time to boil on the outdoor stoves, so we usually arrived very early. Sometimes we would bring a pan of cooked Lasagna that only had to be heated and eaten. (We usually had a barbecue *after* our pasta and meatballs, out of respect for the local customs).

While dinner was cooking we had the games. Softball, if we could keep the men out of their nap chairs and get to the field early enough. Maybe a row on the lake, which was always a treat. Then there was the great Italian game of bocce, or sometimes a set of horseshoes would be produced. One of the reasons these games were such fun is that the adults participated along with the kids. We got to see their more playful sides, but make no mistake, the rules were *enforced*. Cousin Jimmy was very competitive, and he liked to win. That meant every close call in bocce brought out the ruler for a measurement! It also involved a lot of screaming, but of course, being Italians, we didn't notice.

Later in the day, the men would usually get their naps, and the women and children would play cards. In the days before "Game Boy" and text messaging, playing cards was a popular pastime that today is greatly underrated as a social activity. The espresso coffee and Italian pastry came last. The Lagonigros, Bivonas, and Pantalenos were the core families for "Operation Picnic" but often family friends would tag along. As a testament to how much fun was had, we have some wonderful old black and white photos taken with our trusty Kodak "Brownie Camera". Sadly many more photos were lost.

I think we took these family outings for granted because we all lived within blocks of each other and the logistics were so simple. Now our family is scattered all over. A few years back, Cousin Bill and his family hosted a family reunion picnic in New Jersey, and it was a huge success. Cousins who rarely got to see each other had a chance to connect and catch up. It reminded me of just how lucky we were back then to have our family so concentrated in a small geographic area. We grew up with our cousins, aunts and uncles and saw them often. Today we have the memories, and keep in touch by e-mail. Not the same.

Long lost cousins catch up at family reunion

Chapter 26: RADIO CITY MUSIC HALL AND THE AUTOMAT

Back in the Fifties the entertainment scene was much different than today. Sixty-inch wall-mounted plasma TVs, movies recorded on DVDs and downloading tunes to your I-pod were just dreams in the minds of pimply-faced geniuses growing up with no friends. Our main source of entertainment was the movies. Neighborhood theaters were packed with patrons sitting in the darkness mesmerized by the latest Hollywood blockbuster. Movies were also a great place to cool off before air-conditioning in homes was popular. Guys took their girls to the movies so they could sit in the balcony and make out. You could even collect a set of bad dishes a piece at a time on dish nights. But the holy grail of movie theaters, the place everybody in the country wanted to go, was located in Manhattan on Sixth Avenue and 50th Street, the incomparable Radio City Music Hall.

Although this grand theater was not very far from home in Brooklyn, we didn't get there that often. We would usually go during the holidays when they featured their Christmas Spectacular, a first run movie accompanied by a performance by the Rockettes and a stage show that concluded with an on-stage story of the birth of Christ, complete with imaginative sets, lavish costumes and live animals. We were used to the neighborhood Colonial Theater with gum under every seat, so for us Radio City looked like a cathedral. The only movie I remember seeing there was "White Christmas" with Bing Crosby, Danny Kaye, Rosemary Clooney and Vera Ellen. Mom was a huge Bing fan and kept shushing us as we fidgeted in our seats.

We would follow the Music Hall show with a stop at some inexpensive, kid-friendly restaurant like the Automat. Mom would give us each a handful of nickels so we could pick our food, deposit the coins, and open the little glass doors to retrieve our food. For me the food was incidental. The novelty of dropping nickels in a slot and getting food in return was almost too thrilling to bear. My favorites were franks and beans or macaroni and cheese; for dessert it would be Jello or coconut cream pie; and to drink, chocolate milk or, in wintertime, hot chocolate out of a lion's head dispenser. We went home full and happy after these trips, and even a ride on the crowded subway couldn't dampen our spirits.

One thing I remember clearly is that my parents behaved differently toward us and each other on these little outings. Scoldings were minimized, the purse strings were loosened, and there was a lot of laughing and smiling. I don't think I ever appreciated how hard my Mom and dad worked to support us, and didn't realize how much these breaks from the routine must have meant to them. I'm glad Radio City was there to provide some special memories of family time spent together.

Chapter 27: WHERE HAVE YOU GONE, JOE DIMAGGIO

My father Tony was a New York Yankee fan and, from the time he took me to see my first game at Yankee Stadium, I have been too. We walked up the Stadium ramp in the outfield into the bright sunshine. The view that greeted us is still burned into my memory.... emerald green grass, azure blue sky, and there, standing in center field shagging fly balls, was the Yankee Clipper, Joe DiMaggio. Joltin' Joe was in the twilight of his career, but he was my hero.

DiMaggio has been criticized by some as being cool and aloof...not like his more fan friendly teammates Phil Rizzuto or Yogi Berra. So what. Joe played baseball like nobody before or since. His accomplishments speak for themselves: the 56-game hitting streak, the only player in baseball history to be selected for the All-Star Game in every season he played, and his seemingly effortless ability in every aspect of the game: hitting, fielding and base running.

I think the thing that impressed me most as a kid, even more than his physical skills, was the quiet, modest way Joe went about his business. So many of today's athletes are overpaid, substance-abusing, self-promoting jerks who have a couple of good years and think they are God's gift to baseball. Their behavior is embarrassing, and in any baseball clubhouses of the fifties, would have earned them a team beating. The idea of standing at home plate admiring a home run shot would have horrified DiMaggio. Hot dogging was never his style...it was *nobody's* style in the fifties! Guys like Joe, Ted Williams, Jackie Robinson and Willie Mays let their deeds on the field speak for them.

"What's that you say, Mrs. Robinson? Joltin' Joe has left and gone away?" On March 8. 1999, after a debilitating battle with lung cancer, Joe DiMaggio died. The following is taken from his obituary:

"Joe DiMaggio, the fabled slugger and center fielder of the New York Yankees whose superlative play on the baseball field enshrined him in the hearts of sports fans everywhere and made him a universal symbol of athletic grace and excellence, died today at his home in Hollywood, Fla . There was a majesty in his swing, and a self-assured confidence in style and conduct that was uniquely Joe DiMaggio's. In the eye of his public, he was more than a sports hero. He was among the most cherished icons of popular culture."

So long Joe, I feel truly privileged to have seen you play. It was worth all the taunting I got growing up a Yankee fan in Brooklyn.

Chapter 28:   YOU'RE IN THE ARMY NOW

As a kid growing up in Brooklyn, I can remember when neighborhood guys who had joined the military came home on leave, they would walk down the aisle in church on Sunday, all spit and polish, and admiring eyes would turn toward them including mine. So straight out of high school I had no real plan for my life, and with the threat of the draft hanging over me, I joined the Army Reserves in 1960.

Basic training at Fort Dix passed pretty quickly. Come July 4th weekend, our unit was detailed to march that Saturday in a parade in Wildwood, New Jersey. This wasn't quite as good as getting a weekend pass, but it was better than hanging around the base. Our unit was just ahead of the Army Marching Band, and everyone was complaining because were we marching in full dress uniforms in this miserable heat.

As we set off the people pressed forward to watch us go by. The Army Band struck up: "When the Caissons Go Rolling Along". Suddenly there were faces smiling out on us; little kids were running down the sidewalks waving their tiny American flags, and elderly veterans of past wars were holding their hats over their hearts. It was a scene right out of a Norman Rockwell painting.

In an instant, the soldiers all around me stood up straighter and stepped out a little livelier. The complaining stopped because we all had lumps in out throats. Forgotten were the 20-mile night marches with full backpacks, the hours spent shining shoes and polishing brass buckles, even the mean-spirited Sergeants who forced screw-ups to clean latrines with their tooth brushes.

We were soldiers in the United States Army, at that moment feeling honored and privileged to be serving our country.

That's me in the middle flanked by Lefty and Ronnie.

Chapter 29:   TAKE ME WITH YOU, ANGELO

Modern wakes today are boring. They're not even called "wakes" anymore, but the more innocuous "viewings". There was a time when attending an Italian wake was like grand opera. Typically, the wake lasted three full days and was packed with more drama than a week's worth of Law and Order. Three days of organized grieving was a long time for the family of the deceased, especially considering some of the oddballs that would wander in.

In the fifties it was becoming common for wakes to be held in "Funeral Parlors" instead of the homes of the deceased. These establishments were not the elaborate buildings we know today, with cable TV in the lounge and valet parking. Rather they were usually converted residences, and as such, a congregation of smaller rooms. The smell of flowers was overpowering as you entered. Like today, the deceased was at the front of the room in an open coffin...closed coffins were rare except at mob funerals....bullet holes, you know.

For most people, quietly paying your respects to the family, and maybe saying a brief prayer at the casket constituted a "standard grieving visit". For Italians, especially some of the old timers, this wasn't enough. They would make a dramatic entrance, moaning and shrieking even before they left the parking lot. They would then literally hurl themselves toward the casket hollering "Take me with you Angelo, take me with you." (Other visitors at the wake would be hoping that Angelo would somehow grant this request.) As if this wasn't upsetting enough for the family, they would then be subjected to crocodile tears, garlicky kisses and more wailing: "Why him, why poor Angelo". At this point I'd be thinking: "Yeah, why not *YOU*."

Ironically, these blubbery displays would usually be put on by some distant cousin who barely knew the deceased. They were hypocritical "professional mourners" who turned their grief on and off like a faucet. Five minutes later they would be telling jokes to Aunt Tessie in the smoking lounge. At the cemetery, their performance would be repeated. Every family had these mourners with their black dresses pressed and ready to go. Usually, their first words after the deceased was in the ground were: "Where are we eating?"

After attending a funeral, we always headed for Carlucci's Restaurant down the block. As a kid, I think back on our visits to Carlucci's as a "bad news-good news" situation. The bad news is that usually someone had to die for us to go there, but the good news is that we didn't get to eat out restaurants much so you take what you can get. There's a time for grieving and a time for *eating*. The place was plain, but the food was good and plentiful, and served by the always gracious Carlucci family.

Chapter 30:   MY HEROES HAVE ALWAYS BEEN COWBOYS

As a child of the 1950s, I grew up listening to the radio. Some of my favorite shows were cowboy dramas like The Lone Ranger, Hopalong Cassidy and Gene Autry's Melody Ranch..

In the 1950s, the Lone Ranger ruled. He had some good momentum on television from the radio drama. I was glued to my radio at 7:30 pm eagerly anticipating the latest adventures of the masked man and his faithful companion, Tonto. I love modest heroes and the Lone Ranger was as modest as they come. He never stuck around to receive the thanks of the people he helped, but instead left a silver bullet to remember him by. He never killed any bad guys but miraculously shot the guns from their hands. There were many actors who played the Lone Ranger on radio and TV, but I know the true Lone Ranger was Clayton Moore. He had the look, the voice, and the assured presence in the saddle that sent all other pretenders packing.

Another legendary cowboy in the strong, silent mold was James Arness, star of the hit TV series, Gunsmoke. As Marshall Matt Dillon, Arness patrolled the streets of Dodge City in the days of the wild, wild West. The Marshall knew how good he was with a gun, but never flaunted his skill. If anything he was reluctant to get involved in high noon showdowns unless there was no other way. He did his best to reason with the bad guys, but unlike the Lone Ranger, when Matt was forced to draw his six-shooter, he played for keeps. Marshall Dillon was ably assisted by his limping deputy, Chester, and wise old Doc Adams. The love interest on the show was Miss Kitty, owner of the Longbranch Saloon. For some reason it took the Marshall way too long to romance Miss Kitty. Maybe he knew she had been around the corral a few times. Gunsmoke was also a popular radio show with WIlliam Conrad playing Matt Dillon. I suspect that I am the only living person who remembers that.

If I had to pick a more contemporary cowboy hero, it would be Clint Eastwood. Clint played Rowdy Yates on the hit Western TV series Rawhide, but his most memorable strong, silent roles came in the "spaghetti westerns" of the Sixties and Seventies. Classics like "A Fistful of Dollars" and "The Good, The Bad and The Ugly" made a star of Eastwood and launched him into the limelight as the new anti-hero of the old West who didn't always play by the rules. With his flat slouch hat pulled down over his eyes, a cigar stub clenched in his teeth, and a Mexican serape slung over his shoulder, Clint put the fear of God into the black hearts of outlaws before even drawing his gun or casually flipping a lighted stick of dynamite in their direction.

There are others like Gary Cooper, Jimmy Stewart, John Wayne and Steve McQueen who have played the role of the strong, silent cowboy. Me and most guys I grew up with identified with these men and were the ones who went out and faithfully bought Marlboro cigarettes the minute the Marlboro Man rode into our living rooms.

Chapter 31:   THAT LONG WALK ACROSS THE DANCE FLOOR

Most Catholic churches in the fifties held what were called "Confraternity Dances", usually on Friday nights. They were for teens, mostly from the local parish, but some became so successful that outsiders frequently attended. The dances usually featured a live band, and the better-known places like St. Fortunata's church on Linden Blvd. had great Latin bands that went on to achieve fame like Tito Puente and Perez Prado. My friends and I traveled as far as Manhattan and the Bronx to go to places that had the best music, and therefore the best selection of ladies. *Oh yeah.*

We usually traveled in groups of four or five guys. True, it was a dance, but when you ventured outside your home turf, it was nice to know that somebody had your back. The social dynamic at these functions was most interesting. Usually the girls would sit on one side of the dance floor and the boys on the other. Asking a girl to dance required a long walk across the dance floor (in full view of all assembled) and running the risk of getting shot down in flames. This is the true meaning of courage because the walk back was a lot longer. Guys tended to set their sights low early in the evening, and only if they were rewarded with some success, did they aim higher.

One of the biggest assets in our group was my buddy Phil. He was not only tall and good looking, but unlike the rest of us, had taught himself how to dance from watching American Bandstand on television. (This was a great show with Dick Clark that featured Philadelphia teens dancing on-camera, with guest appearances by the up and coming rock and roll artists of the day.) The kids on the show were regulars, and soon became so popular that they had a following all their own. Anyhow, Phil was our *babe magnet*, and the rest of us were like the fish known as "remora" who attach themselves to sharks and feed off the leavings of the shark's meals.

Once Phil had established a beach head, the rest of the landing party would bring up the rear. Usually the girls he danced with had friends who mistakenly assumed we could all dance like Phil. Imagine their surprise when they discovered what "spastics" we were. It required some fast talking and no small amount of charm to overcome our "terpsicorically challenged" performances on the dance floor. Phil was our "Trojan Horse", there to lure the unsuspecting ladies into our waiting arms.

We dressed in jackets and sometimes neckties for these dances. (This was back before people appeared in public in pajama bottoms and ratty t-shirts.) Being on limited budgets, there was one shameless fashion trick we used to make our wardrobes more appealing; when men's crew-neck sweaters came into vogue, we simply took our old V-neck sweaters and wore them *backwards*. This clever deception was never noticed since we typically wore jackets over our sweaters, Hey, it's a meat market out there, and we had to compete.

Our feelings and behavior toward the opposite sex were so naive and klutzy. This was a whole new universe for teen boys with raging hormones and absolutely no clue about how to talk to girls. Nothing in our experience prepared us for socializing with young ladies who, for some reason, were not bowled over by our sure-fire "pull my finger" gag. Luckily, the girls knew what freaks we were, and treated us like wild beasts who could be tamed with kindness and soothing words.

Chapter 32:   CHRISTMAS IN THE HOOD

Christmas was always a special time for families in our Brooklyn neighborhood. It was probably the one time that people who watched their pennies all year splurged without guilt. For us kids, it wasn't just about the presents. There was a whole different feel in the air...an excited hustle and bustle as everyone rushed around buying and decorating trees, shopping for food and gifts, building snow forts, and of course, buying out the fish store for the traditional, Italian Christmas Eve Feast of the Seven Fishes.

A word about Christmas trees. Back then there were no "tree farms" whose sole crop was fat, perfectly shaped Christmas trees delivered just in time for the holidays. Trees were usually scrawny affairs, with sparse sections that had to be turned toward the wall so that they wouldn't show so much. My father was not so accepting of nature's imperfect Christmas trees. He would drill holes into the trunk of the tree and insert extra branches to fill out its shape. There is a famous poem by Joyce Kilmer that concludes with the lines: "Poems are made by fools like me, but only God can make a tree". I guess Pop never read that one.

Christmas Eve was spent at Grandma and Grandpa Camardi's house on Hull Street. Fried zeppoles were a special treat. After being cooked in a large tub of hot oil they were sprinkled with powdered sugar. Christmas day itself was the same then as for kids today...fevered excitement. We had to wait until Christmas morning to open our gifts. As I think back, I don't remember ever being disappointed. I now realize how much my parents had to sacrifice to get the three of us what we really wanted, and love them all the more for it. Later that day we would gather at Aunt Anna's and eat like the Russians were in Newark. Italians ate the equivalent of at least three dinners on holidays.

My final Christmas memory is of borderline arson. People didn't keep their trees very long in those days. They dried out and became dangerous. One or two days after Christmas, trees would be put out for collection by the Sanitation Department, unless we beat them to it. We would gather up all the trees we could find and pile them up in a vacant lot across the street from my house. (You see of course where this is going.) After a while we had a crackling blaze going, with flames three stories high. Young boys are fascinated with fire, and we just kind of stood around watching it burn out.

It seems like maybe three months between Christmases these days. Growing older means that time moves along at warp speed. Watching "Its a Wonderful Life" every year reminds me that I've been blessed with a great family, and nothing gives me more pleasure than spending the holidays with them.

Chapter 33:   THE NEIGHBORHOOD SOCIAL CLUB

Thanks to shows like "The Sopranos", people sometimes to tag all neighborhood social clubs with the "mob hangout" label. While it can't be denied that some of them shielded criminals and mob activities, the vast majority of them were harmless havens where men could gather, play cards and enjoy a glass of wine free from the intrusions of the outside world. Every Brooklyn neighborhood had a Democrat or Republican Club that offered opportunities to socialize.

We had at least two such clubs in the neighborhood...one on Fulton Street and another on Pitkin Avenue. Typically they were storefronts with tables and chairs (rescued from the garbage) set up outside for the members to sit at and enjoy their espresso laced with Anisette. Except for the coldest days, the doors were always open and sometimes music, usually Sinatra or opera, could be heard coming from inside. Many of the men lounging around were Italian, reflecting the population of the area. Some looked dapper in double-breasted suits and Boston Blackie pencil moustaches. Others were more casual in worn trousers and "pizza man" undershirts. They all had one thing in common: they looked slightly sinister and were highly suspicious of outsiders.

Despite this unsavory image, Italian men are really highly social and the atmosphere in these clubs was always gregarious. There was usually a game of Briscola (an Italian card game played in deadly earnest) in progress. Overheard snatches of conversations might include references to the Brooklyn Dodgers, the pros and cons of 'Neopolitan' vs.Sicilian pizza, what horse looked good in the third at Belmont, how Vito caught his wife with the grocery boy, "that bastard Kennedy", and a hundred other topics from the ridiculous to the sublime. Each club had at least one bookie who would take bets on the daily number, horse races, ball games, or even the color of the next car coming down the street.

Kids were usually chased away unless there was an errand to be run. "Hey kid, go get me a slice and an orange soda" or "...go ring my bell and ask my wife if she needs me to pick up anything on the way home." There was usually a nickel or dime in it for us to carry out these assignments, and we did so gladly. We would sometimes go to the club on Sunday mornings with our shoe shine boxes knowing the guys liked to dress up. Polished, "french toe" shoes were a must with pegged pants.

On rare occasions we were invited inside for a cold drink or to settle an argument. "Hey kid, tell this moron the capital of New Jersey ain't Newark." The movie "A Bronx Tale" was so compelling because it captured perfectly these strange connections between neighborhood kids and grown men of respect in Italian-American neighborhoods.

The thought of 10-year-old boys going into clubs with grown men would strike terror into the hearts of today's parents. Nobody gave it much thought back then. Your mother would say: "I don't want you hanging around that club. Those men are a bad influence." We would nod 'yes' and head straight for the club; how could they stop us. It's not that we didn't love our mothers and listen to a lot of the advice they gave, it's just that we knew there was no other honest way to make two dollars or more on a Sunday morning. I realized some of these guys were not role models, but they weren't The Sopranos either. I never heard any murders or kidnappings plotted; the worst you might get is yelled at for getting shoe polish on some guy's white sock. I sometimes even heard: "Hey, watch your mouth, there's a kid here."

Let's face it...neighborhood social clubs are the poor man's version of the universally accepted, even admired, private clubs on Wall Street. Although the incomes of the members might vary widely, the aims of these clubs are the same: to have a place where a guy can go to have a drink in peace, kid around with his friends, and get away from "the pld ball and chain" for a few hours.

Chapter 34: UNCLE NICK

Uncle Nick Bivona married my mother's sister Mary. Because the whole family lived near one another in Brooklyn during the 1950s, I saw a lot of Uncle Nick. He was one of the most easy-going men I ever met. He must have got angry sometime, but I never saw it. He was always the one who led the car caravans on the family picnics we enjoyed. The cars followed the white handkerchief tied to the radio antenna of his car,

Nick was a U.S. Navy veteran who fathered three children, Millie, Nick Jr. and Sal. Although tall and trim, I never saw a man who could eat like Uncle Nick. He and Aunt Mary were the adventurers in the family. In those days people were pretty conservative, having grown up in a time when money was always tight. If you had a job and a steady income, most men were content with their lot. Nick earned his living as a "presser", I assume in some type of garment factory.

That didn't stop him and Aunt Mary from starting a number of business to try to improve their lot. One I remember distinctly was a dressmaking shop on Fulton Street. I believe they had an apartment above the shop, the windows of which were not far from the elevated tracks of the subway. Whenever the trains rumbled by the furniture inside the apartment would move along the polished wood floor.

Nick moved his family to the wilds of Selden, Long Island in the early 1960s. The three-bedroom house cost under $6,000 in the days when there were still wild Indians roaming the plains of Long Island. They lived there for many years until moving south after their retirement. He was a kind and loving man who served as a role model for me and my cousins.

Uncle Nick and Aunt Mary's wedding

Chapter 35: SATURDAY AFTERNOONS IN THE DARK

As a child, going to the movies was an all day affair. We arrived at the Colonial Theater on Broadway around 11 a.m. prepared for a full day of entertainment. Popcorn would never sustain us...we carried pepper and egg "sangwiches" in oily brown bags. After paying the 14 cent admission price, we found our seats. As we got older, we always tried to sneak over to the "adult" seats, but the usher or "Matron" as she was called then invariably shooed us back to the kids' section. The Saturday viewing lineup usually started with the Movietone News. This was a black and white newsreel that trumpeted the events of the day. It featured the familiar voice of Lowell Thomas. Also covered was sports, with the great Bill Stern.

Then came the cartoons....21 of them to be exact. Don't ask me where they came up with 21; all I know is that if you were in the audience of the Colonial Theater on Saturday, you were seeing 21 cartoons. Sometimes they would end the cartoon-fest with a sing-along, where the audience followed the bouncing ball as it skipped across the lyrics to the song on the screen. By now the "sangwiches" were gone and a trip to the candy counter was needed.

There was always a movie "serial" which was an action-adventure film that was shown in chapters. Each week a new chapter would be screened, with a cliff-hanging ending that left you gasping for more. Some of the serials I remember are Buster Crabbe in "Flash Gordon" (a futuristic space travel theme with special effects that were comical); and Gene Autry in The "Thunder Riders" (a bunch of kids who resembled the Dead End kids out West).

Wait, wasn't there a movie? Oh yeah, there were *two movies*, a *main* feature and what was called a *"B"* feature. The main feature probably lasted no more than 90 minutes, and the B picture even less. They told their stories with no nonsense, and on budgets that wouldn't cover the director's massages on one of today's drawn-out epics.

Forgive me if I use the word "magical", but a day at the movies *was* magical to us. Classics like Bambi, Song of the South, High Noon, From Here to Eternity and so many others kept us mesmerized in our seats. And don't forget, Monday was free dish night.

Chapter 36: MY CAREER AS A CHOIR BOY

When I hear singing in church, I think back to my days in the choir at Our Lady of Lourdes in Brooklyn. The choir was made up of school boys and neighborhood men under the direction of Brother Justinian, the school principal. He was a big man in dark robes with jet black hair combed straight back. I think Darth Vader was modeled after him.

For us boys, the auditions for the choir were not voluntary. Every year, Brother Justinian gathered the classes from school in his office and we all sang aloud. He went around and bent his ear to hear each boy. If he liked what he heard, you were in the choir. Period. The high point of every year for the choir was Christmas Eve Mass. The church was massive but it was not easy finding a seat. People came from other parishes just to hear us sing.

As seen in the picture, the choir loft at Our Lady of Lourdes was in the rear of the church, reached by a long staircase. All year long we rehearsed for the Christmas Eve service, and now stood in rows in our white shirts and blue ties waiting for Brother sitting at the grand organ to give us our cue. I wish I had a recording of how good we sounded. Many of the traditional carols were sung, some in Latin. I still remember those lyrice to this day.

After Mass the people filed out into the cold night to go home and maybe open some early presents. We came down last, and Brother Justinian waited at the door to present each boy with a big box of Whitman's Sampler chocolates. He worked us hard but you could see the pride in his eyes when we performed. Sometimes before we rehearsed, he'd sit at the piano in his office and riff jazz tunes. It gives me a nice feeling to think of those days and how lucky I was to be raised in that time and place.

Chapter 37:   THE DREAM BIKE

As a boy in Brooklyn, you knew you had arrived when you rode a Schwinn Black Phantom bike. In the Fifties, this was a kid's two-wheeled equivalent of a Corvette. It was red, black and gold, with tons of chrome. Kids would fasten playing cards with a clothespin to the bike's frame so that they hit the spokes as the wheels turned, making a loud noise that was supposed to sound like a motorcycle....too cool for words. We also attached streamers to the handle bars, extra lights and chrome crossbars to really pimp that ride.

Most of us couldn't afford the dream bike. I learned to ride on an old girl's bike handed down from my cousin Joan. Training wheels hadn't been invented yet, and skinned shins were the badge of honor for learning to ride a two-wheeler. I can remember my father "Tony Boots" teaching me to ride...we would go to the playground and he would run alongside me in his ever present suit, tie and snappy fedora, usually with a Lucky Strike in his mouth. In reality, I was happy to have any bike at all since money was tight and we could never afford anything close to the Schwinn dream bike. Then Fate intervened.

There was an old TV show called "Junior Champions", hosted by the great broadcaster, Marty Glickman. I was lucky enough to be chosen to represent my day camp, JHS 73, and competed in a contest to see who could shoot and hit the most layups in one minute. I won, and with a hard cast on my broken left wrist. (Thank you, thank you very much.) The winner's prize was a new Shelby bike. Now maybe Shelby was to Schwinn what Timex was to Rolex, but what the hell, I had a brand new bike. Except for my pal Johnny, who rode a Schwinn thanks to his father who ran the local barber shop and bookie joint, I had the best bike in the neighborhood. Sweet.

PS I now ride a new Schwinn bike, but it's like running into an old girlfriend after 50 years....just not the same.

Chapter 38: IT'S HOWDY DOODY TIME

We got our first black and white TV, a 17-inch RCA console, probably in the mid-fifties. In our viewing area we received just seven channels, 2, 4, 5, 7, 9, 11 and 13. There was an antenna on the roof and/or a pair of "rabbit ears" on top of the television to help improve reception. I can honestly say there were more shows worth watching on those lousy seven channels than on the one thousand channels I get today. The weekly schedule didn't change all that much and we didn't want it to...every family had its favorite shows, and they came on the same time every week.

Comedy was king in the fifties, with Milton Berle leading the pack. Other great comedy shows featured Sid Caesar in Your Show of Shows, The Jack Benny Show, The Red Skelton Show, and You Bet Your Life with Groucho Marx. Although Milton was king, my two "personal best" awards would go to Jackie Gleason's Honeymooners and I Love Lucy with the brilliant Lucille Ball. These two shows, unlike some of the others, are timeless and just as funny today as back then.

Westerns too had a strong run. Shows like Wagon Train, The Lone Ranger, Hopalong Cassidy, Gunsmoke, Rawhide, Gene Autry and Death Valley Days. Every kid wanted to be a cowboy. TV quiz shows like The $64,000 Question (remember the isolation booth), Twenty One and Tic Tac Dough were a sensation until the roof came crashing down. The gravy train derailed in September of 1958 when disgruntled former show contestants went public with accusations that the results were rigged and the contestants coached.

Ed Sullivan, Perro Como, Dinah Shore, Martin and Lewis...all these personalities and more hosted TV Variety shows. The format was a popular one with guest stars of the day making appearances with the host. The longest running variety show in history was Ed Sullivan's Toast of the Town which ran from 1948 to 1971. Ed looked like he had just been embalmed, but the man knew talent. Headliners like Elvis, The Beatles, The Rolling Stones, Sonny and Cher, The Smothers Brothers, and many more, made their careers on Sunday nights at 8 o'clock.

For the young, we had kiddy shows from the primitive Junior Frolics with Uncle Fred on Channel 13 to the sublime Wonderful World of Disney. This series spawned the Davy Crockett craze of 1955 with the miniseries about the historical American frontiersman, starring Fess Parker in the title role. Millions of dollars in merchandise were sold relating to the title character, and every boy wanted a coonskin cap for Christmas. Disney also gave us the Mickey Mouse Club, which brainwashed millions of "Mouseketeers" to pester their parents for a trip to Disney's theme parks, which were just getting off the ground. Other popular shows were Howdy Doody, Captain Video, Lassie and Captain Kangaroo.

Last but not least came the family sitcoms....big ratings getters in the fifties with shows like Make Room for Daddy (Danny Thomas), Father Knows Best (Robert Young), Burns and Allen, Amos and Andy, Ozzie and Harriet, My Little Margie, Our Miss Brooks and literally dozens more. The fifties were the golden age for TV sitcoms. They had a quality of innocence about them...controversy was avoided at all costs with the object being to simply entertain. Some of my fondest family memories are of sitting together with the whole family and laughing at these great shows.

Understand that television was a big deal for us. There were no computers, video games, cell phones or I-pods. For children of the radio generation, TV was a wondrous gift from on high.

Who cared that it wasn't color, high definition, plasma or surround-sound; we sat around that flickering black and white screen like cavemen around the first fire.

Chapter 39: SUMMER DAY CAMP

From the time I was about 10, and for three or four years thereafter, I attended summer day camp at Junior High School 73, on MacDougal Street in Brooklyn. My mother went to the school as a girl as did her famous classmate, the Great One, Jackie Gleason. Summer Camp for kids today usually means some serene, bucolic place in the country, with dorms, counselors and singing songs around the campfire. My summer camp was the city version...concrete, brick buildings and traffic whizzing by on Rockaway Avenue.

I really didn't want to go, after all, summer was *my time*; no school, no homework and out in the street from dawn to dusk. I'm sure this is what worried my mother. She couldn't watch me every minute, and for sure I was a handful at that age. We would ride our bikes from my block in Brooklyn to Howard Beach in Queens, a distance of about five miles along some of the busiest streets you can imagine. Clearly, Mom wanted me under closer supervision.

Once at summer camp, I flat-out loved it. What kid wouldn't. They had other kids my age to play with, a great arts and crafts program (to this day I can weave a mean lanyard) and best of all, SPORTS. Every day we got to play softball or football in the school yard. They had organized track and field competitions in which I eagerly participated. Their sports program was run by a man named Norm Drucker whose full-time job was refereeing in the National Basketball Association. I guess the pay for refs was so poor in those days that he had to supplement his income with a summer job. Or maybe he just wanted to help city kids stay off the streets.

During those years there was a TV show called Junior Champions hosted by Marty Glickman, the great Olympic athlete and sportscaster. They selected kids from local day camps to come on the show and compete for prizes. I had recently fractured my left wrist in a camp high jump event, and was sporting a hard cast on my left arm.

While waiting to go on camera, all the kids who were competing were being briefed by a staff person on what to do while on-camera. I guess I was around 12 at the time, a raging pile of adolescent hormones. Anyhow, the person briefing us was a tall, stunning redhead. After talking to the group, she came over, sat down next to me, and put her arm around my shoulder. I could feel the blood rush to my cheeks. She looked at me and began speaking: "You want to be a hit on the show, don't you?" she asked. "Y-y-y-yes" I stammered" She went on: "You want your family and friends to be proud of you" she whispered into my ear. "Y-y-y-yes" again was my clever reply. "Then you'd better zip up your fly" said red.

No hole was deep enough for me to crawl into. That was my first brush with women; it's a miracle I didn't enter the priesthood then and there.

A belated "Thank You" to men like Norm Drucker and Marty Glickman who helped make summers memorable for boys like me. As for that redhead, well I forgive you, but I hope you never need a kidney.

P.S. I spoke to Norm Drucker a few years back. He had retired to Florida and was very gracious when I reminded him how much he did for Brooklyn kids. He has since passed. R.I.P. Mr. Drucker.

Chapter 40: HOW I LEARNED TO CURSE

When I was a kid, model trains were on every boy's Christmas list. I had the Marx Standard gauge set, but later as an adult, switched to the Lionel HO gauge just to save space. I remember as a kid, we would set the trains up around the tree every Christmas. My father would lay down the track that had to be nailed to a plywood board. Things didn't always go smoothly with the set up and I learned to string together curse words as my dad struggled to get it right. Looking back, I think one of the reasons I loved these trains so much is that working on them was one of the few things my Dad and I got to do together. He worked two jobs to pay the mortgage, so I valued any time he had to spend with me.

Once the metal tracks were down, we would lightly sandpaper them to ensure the train wheels encountered no friction in their trip around Tiny Town. We then set out the model buildings including the post office, general store, Woolworths and the bank. We had specialty trains like the cattle car that required a trackside platform accessory where the cows could be offloaded using magnets to move them jerkily along. We also had a water tower that loomed over the tracks and was used to simulate filling the black metal locomotive with water. Of course there were Styrofoam tunnels for the locomotive and its trailing freight cars to pass through, and an electric gate that came down automatically to block traffic while the train roared by.

Once the trains and layout were set up, my Dad's job was done and the trains were mine. Just watching them go round and round became boring after 30 seconds, and so I released my imagination to liven things up. I would take some logs from the log car, lay them across the track, and use them to help masked outlaws derail the train so they could rob it. I also like to see how fast the train could go in reverse before it careened off the tracks and took out the post office. Sometimes I would use my little, plastic cowboy and Indian figures to stage epic battles where brave lawmen would jump down onto the moving train from the top of the Styrofoam tunnel to fight the murderous redskins who had boarded the train with mayhem in mind. (I usually waited until Dad was out before doing this stuff or he would have brained me.)

Today's kids know computers and electronic games, but I really think the toys we played with in the 50's required more imagination. The only store on Staten Island that sold model railroad trains and accessories closed a few years ago. The owner offered me a good deal on the stuff he was selling, but I politely declined explaining that my railroad days were behind me. I used to set the trains up every year for a time, but my own kids seemed more interested in Transformer action figures than model trains.

Once in a while I get to a train show in Manhattan, and there is always the great model train display at Northlandz in Flemington, New Jersey that has floors and floors of layouts. Model railroading was great fun for me, both as a kid and an adult, but most important, it gave me some quality time with my Dad, something I will always cherish.

Chapter 41: CONFESSIONS OF AN 11 YEAR OLD SMOKER

Smoking was considered cool back in the Fifties. Movie stars, athletes, nearly everyone lit 'em up. There were even cigarette ads with doctors endorsing one brand or other for its healthful, relaxing benefits. It was only natural then that kids would become curious about smoking and want to emulate the adults around them.

My Dad smoked Luckies before filtered cigarettes hit the market. I was probably around 11 when I first snuck one out of his pack. We would usually go off to Callahan-Kelly Park for our clandestine puffs, far away from the prying eyes of the "block watchers"...older women who would rat us out to our own parents for any indiscretion. By age 12 we were buying our own. At 25 cents a pack, it was no hardship. Cigarettes today cost close to ten bucks a pack. My Dad knew I smoked and would sometimes bum one from me...sadly, they proved to be his undoing, dying of lung cancer at age 72.

Cigarettes were boldly advertised in the fifties. There were ashtrays in every room of every house. Unlike today when smokers have to sneak into an alley for their fix, smoking was permitted everywhere: airplanes, office buildings, theaters, even hospital rooms; you were free to have a smoke pretty much anywhere. Of course a pack of cigarettes cost about a quarter back then, so two packs a day was no big financial burden. The last time I checked, to buy a carton of cigarettes you needed a co-signer for the loan.

Ad agencies were at their creative best when selling cigarettes. Some of the more memorable ads used well known celebrities like Lucile Ball, Arthur Godfrey and future President Ronald Reagan. One of the most successful and long-running ad campaigns was for Marlboro. The "Marlboro Man" became the new yardstick for manly good looks. Guys who smoked Marlboros could identify with the rugged cowboys of the old West. I dumped my old brand in a heartbeat to proudly join the swelling ranks of the Marlboro Men.

I know it's not a popular notion today, but I enjoyed smoking. There was nothing like a cigarette with my morning coffee or after a satisfying meal. If they could figure out a way to make cigarettes harmless, I'd run out and buy a carton of Marlboros in a minute. That is if I could get a co-signer for the loan.

Chapter 42:   UNCLE MIKE

Back in 2013 my Uncle Mike passed away. He would have turned 90 that May. Michael was my mother's younger brother and the last of the children born to Pasquale and Caterina Camardi. That's him with my mom at the 1939 New York World's Fair. He was a cool character blessed with dark good looks complete with a pencil-thin mustache that he wore all his life. I remember at our Christmas and New Year's Eve family parties when he was still single he would always show up with a lovely girl on his arm to spend some time with the family before going off for the evening's entertainment.

As a young man, Uncle Mike liked living large, even when his income didn't support it. He always dressed impeccably and carried himself like an Italian Count. He drove nice cars and went to nice places despite a less than stable financial foundation. I remember overhearing the family discussing his lavish (to them) lifestyle and his reluctance to put his nose to the grindstone and settle down with a nice Italian girl. Once he borrowed my mother's movie projector to show some stag films at a bachelor party. In with the projector was a reel of old film of my parents wedding, a gift from Negri's Furniture, a neighborhood store that filmed your nuptials if you bought furniture there. Sadly the film was lost and Uncle Mike was in my mom's doghouse for a long time. I can't blame her; I'd give a lot to still have that rare film of my folks.

In his 30's Uncle Mike was seriously dating a girl named Ella. She was pretty, vivacious and got on famously with the family. We thought for sure that this was "the one". The next thing we knew there was an engagement announcement, but Ella was not the lucky girl. Uncle Mike had met an attorney named Lola and decided to marry her. Her family was well off and apparently happy to have Mike in the fold. I remember going to their wedding. It was probably the first "catered affair" I had ever attended (see photo) where dinner was served by waiters instead of the football weddings we were used to. It was nothing like the elaborate weddings of today, but for poor Brooklyn Italians, it was "tre elegante".

The marriage turned out to be the best thing that ever happened to Mike. Aunt Lola was a smart, ambitious woman who would never tolerate a lay-about husband. With her prodding and connections, Uncle Mike crashed the business world and became a purchasing agent for a trucking company. From these humble beginnings he rose steadily in the company, apparently having a natural gift for schmoozing and a good business sense. He worked for many years until finally retiring when he was around 80! Grandma and Grandpa would have been proud to see their son, over whose future they had so needlessly fretted, become a real force in the business community. Uncle Mike also adopted a son, Michael, from Lola's previous marriage, who turned out to be a successful doctor with a practice in Virginia.

A few years ago I was compiling a family history, and Uncle Mike was kind enough to share his written recollections of the old days on Hull Street. There were some lovely details about my grandparents' early lives and Mike's sisters including my mother that I was able to share with my children. We said goodbye at a small service in Roslyn Heights where Uncle Mike lived. Most of our remaining family members are no longer living in New York, so my sister, my wife and I attended to represent the family. I will celebrate Mike's life and remember him as he would wish to be remembered...a guy who loved life and squeezed all he could out of it.

Uncle Mike with my mom (his sister) at the 1939 World's Fair

Family pic taken I believe at Mike and Lola's wedding

(Me sitting, second from left)

Chapter 43: VITO, THROW ME A CAPICOLA

Before we were so consumed with outdoing one another, weddings were much more modest affairs. Back in the fifties, Brooklyn Italians were famous for throwing "football weddings". I'm not sure where the term originated, but at these weddings, the food was simple fare, mostly cold-cut sandwiches wrapped in wax paper. Each table would have a pile of sandwiches, and if you didn't find something you liked, it was common to holler across the room: "Hey Vito, throw me a capicola", at which point Vito would comply and sail the sandwich through the air to whoever requested it. At the height of the meal, the scene would resemble a football game with the air filled with flying salami or ham and cheese sandwiches.

These affairs were typically held in a hall rented out by organizations like the American Legion or the Knights of Columbus. There was a polished wood dance floor surrounded by folding tables and chairs. Kids were usually invited to weddings since it didn't cost $500 per guest. A big thrill for us kids was to get a running start and to slide as far as we could across the polished floor. You would be hard-pressed to find a margarita-dispensing fountain at these functions, but there was plenty of beer in pitchers, and at high-class affairs, a bottle of scotch or rye on each table. Music was provided by local talent; the band almost always included an accordion.

As the evening progressed and the level in the scotch and rye bottles diminished, the fun would begin in earnest. There was an uncle in every family whose hobby it was to get blotto at weddings and disgrace himself, usually winding up driving the porcelain bus in the men's room. Men began to dance, not with their wives, but with each other. My father "Tony Boots" had a routine that never varied; he would tie his jacket around his waist like a hula skirt, and then swish a cloth napkin back and forth across his derriere in what was probably the worst imitation of a strip tease ever. Bonus laughs might be had if one of the kids sliding across the dance floor collided with Tony in mid-swish.

Toward the end of the evening, the bride and groom would make their rounds of the tables to collect the "busta", an Italian term for wedding envelope. Usually it was cash or, for the more upwardly mobile pisani, a check. (Some seasoned wedding-goers would not seal the gift envelope until they were satisfied that the party was worth the twenty bucks they put in. If the event was not up to their expectations, then ten bucks would discretely be removed. This is another New York custom...giving money as a wedding gift. In other parts of the country, people give punch bowls, 3-D pictures of horses, or re-gifted gravy boats. I think the Italians got it right...keep the crap and show me the money every time.

People today might be horrified to hear how these weddings went, but you know what, they'd be wrong. We had wonderful times at these football weddings and it didn't require you to mortgage your house to pay for one. Given the choice between today's extravaganzas and the simple parties in the American Legion halls, I can only say: "Hey Vito, throw me a capicola".

My parents were married on September 24, 1940

Fran and Tony's wedding invitation, September 24, 1940

Mr. and Mrs. Pasquale Camardi
Mrs. Lucia Pontelиana
request the honor of your presence
at the marriage of their children

Frances

to

Anthony

Sunday, September 29th, 1940
at 6:00 p. m.

at Our Lady of Loretto Church
Sackman & Pacific Sts., Brooklyn, N. Y.

Reception at Brooklyn Palace
Rockaway Ave. bet. Hull & Somers St., Bklyn
at 7:00 p. m.

Bride's Res: 2402 Dean St., Brooklyn

Chapter 44:   TEN CENTS AND A DREAM

This is about a magic carpet ride that only cost a dime: the comic book. In the dark days before television, computers and video games, kids had few options outside their own imaginations, to help them fantasize. I'm not saying that was a bad thing, quite the contrary, a fertile imagination can open the door to new worlds for young and curious minds. Maybe that's why comic books were so popular with children of my generation. They gave us new doors and new worlds to peek behind, allowing our imaginations to do the rest.

If you didn't grow up loving comic books, as I did, it will be hard for you to understand what they meant to me. The first level of appreciation came from my physical senses. The candy stores where they were sold displayed comic books arranged neatly on shelves so that the titles could be read. They had glossy, brilliantly illustrated covers that shouted their titles: Archie and Veronica, Little Lulu, Red Ryder, Superman, Batman, Lash Larue, Donald Duck...all familiar characters to comic lovers. We stood mesmerized, shiny dime clutched in sweaty palms, eyeballing the new arrivals to see which would come home with us. It took a while.

Once we got our treasure home, the sense of smell kicked in. Nothing smelled like a newly opened comic book. Whether it was the paper, the ink or both, we inhaled that smell like older guys who experience the rapture of that first new car smell. Maybe there's a connection. Since new comics were *always* read in private, we could enjoy the smell without people looking funny at us. Once a new comic had been read, it was as if something went out of it. It sat there begging to be read again, but it wasn't the same comic anymore.

Other than stimulating the senses, comics took you away. They made you laugh, sucked you into great adventures, and generally stretched the limits of 'the possible.' We knew they weren't real, but for fifteen minutes or so, we allowed ourselves to go along. We shook our heads at Uncle Scrooge's miserly ways, marveled at Lash Larue's skill with a bullwhip, and worried ourselves sick as Superman unwittingly exposed himself to Lex Luthor's kryptonite trap. Today, preserving comics in plastic sleeves and hoarding them as collectibles is in fashion. We put them to better use, sitting on the stoop and trading them among ourselves to get comics you wanted to read, but not badly enough to part with a dime.

Comics were also the gateway to miracle products that would change your life. Charles Atlas invented the dynamic tension system to help build up muscles on skinny guys so they wouldn't get sand kicked in their faces at the beach while their girlfriends laughed. How about the pet monkey that was almost human and, for the paltry price of $18.99, would be mailed to you from the Animal Farm in Miami, live delivery guaranteed. All boys, if they had two dollars, would send away for the amazing X-ray vision glasses that allowed you to see through anything. The leer on the face of the kid wearing them in the ad told us all we needed to know.

They still sell comics today, but they can't compete with Wii or X-Box for kids' attention. For me, that shoe box full of comics under my bed was my 'open sesame' to escape the streets of Brooklyn for a little while.

Chapter 45:   LUCKY STRIKE LANES

Before HDTVs, multiplex cinemas, and smart phones, there was bowling. In the 1950s, bowling was really coming on strong, although it peaked in the 1960s, with about 14,000 across the country. They even televised early bowling matches with pro-legends like Carmen Salvino and Dick Weber. Bowling was popular because it didn't require any special equipment, was relatively cheap, and something families could do together. It was also a popular activity for first dates. The rapid growth of television put a lot of neighborhood movie theaters out of business, and in their places sprang up bowling alleys. Our alley of choice was Lucky Strike Lanes on Atlantic Avenue and Crescent Street.

Lucky Strike was an older bowling alley that looked run down compared to the newer, modern alleys being built. It was so old that for a while they had lanes set aside for Duckpins, a form of bowling that uses smaller pins and a smaller ball. This was the game that Rip Van Winkle is reputed to have invented, and I wouldn't be surprised if Rip rolled a few games at Lucky Strike. When we first started bowling there, they still had pin boys who would climb up on a ledge behind the bowling pins and manually reset the pins after each frame. Most of them were not boys but hard drinking men who probably couldn't get any other work.

Lucky Strike had a snack stand and a bar that sold beer and soft drinks. I think beers were fifteen cents a glass, and every few frames someone would holler out "beer frame", and whoever had the worst score that frame was shamed into buying the next round. You would think that, understandably, after a few beery games like this, scores would begin to decline. The lanes were so old though, that after tens of thousands of heavy balls rolling toward the pocket, there was an indentation worn into the wood such that any ball drunkenly flung down the alley would settle into this groove and voilà, a strike.

At some point we formed a team and even got a sponsor, a neighborhood Hoffman soda distributor. Our team shirts were a cream color with the sponsors name written in green letters on the back. (Yes, that's me at around age 16, before my back gave out.) We couldn't afford to buy our own custom-drilled balls so we had to use whatever house balls were on the racks. It was a bummer if you got there and somebody had already claimed your ball. Eventually I found a ladies' ball that fit me pretty well, and I could always be sure of finding it since it was a lovely lavender color. We rented shoes for fifteen cents; no extra charge for the fungus. We had a couple of good bowlers, but most of the teams in the league were comprised of older men who bowled us under the table.

When the nicer lanes appeared, sadly, Lucky Strike closed its doors. Guys wanted to take their girls to the gleaming chrome and neon palaces opening in Brooklyn like Maple Lanes on 60th Street and Gil Hodges Lanes in Mill Basin. Games were only a quarter back then, so for around five bucks you and your date were good to go for a night of entertainment including bowling and food. We would often go with groups of guys, and sometimes a few girls would join in. It allowed us to mingle with the opposite sex without the pressure of going on a "date".

My granddaughter likes to bowl, and the alleys today are great with kids. They have ramps to roll the balls down so they have enough speed to make it to the pins. They also use bumpers near the gutters so kids don't throw gutter balls. They are fabulous places with indirect lighting, full restaurants, automated, electronic scoring, and not a pin boy in sight.

Me in action at Lucky Strike Lanes

Chapter 46:   TO THE MOON, ALICE

To this day my favorite sitcom ever is The Honeymooners, especially the episodes known as "the classic 39" that spanned the 1955-56 seasons of the show.

Jackie Gleason drew heavily on his reminiscences of growing up on Chauncey Street in Brooklyn. The main characters are based on people he knew who worked hard while chasing their small dreams. Ralph Kramden reminded me of my father, Tony Boots, whose next big deal was always just around the corner. His hobbies included betting on slow horses and picking bad stocks.

My mother was his Alice Kramden, always trying to talk sense into him and being there to pick up the pieces until the next big thing came along. Meanwhile she found a way to keep food on the table and clothes on our backs with a paycheck that was never enough. Like Ralph Kramden, my dad knew he had "married up" and was crazy about my mother. All his schemes were intended to make a better life for her.

My three favorite episodes:

Better Living Through Television: Ralph chases another get-rich quick scheme and ropes in poor Norton. They decide to sell a multi-purpose kitchen utensil and, to drum up business, go on TV with a commercial starring Ralph and Ed. While rehearsing the commercial extolling the virtues of the product, Ralph is his usual blustering self, telling Norton how to act and to follow his lead. Naturally, when they go live on-camera, Norton is flawless while Ralph turns into a stuttering zombie. Watching him break out in flop sweat and bumble through the commercial ("It can core a apple") is not only funny, but it strikes a note of recognition for anyone who ever had to deliver that big presentation or speak in public for the first time.

Brother Ralph: Ralph is laid off, and Alice decides to take a job as a secretary, but has to tell her boss that Ralph is her *brother* since companies usually don't hire married women. House-husband Ralph is not thrilled when Alice's boss turns out to be a handsome hunk named Tony. Ralph insists that any overtime be done at home where he can chaperon. The show is funny enough, but for me the biggest laugh came early in the show when Ralph comes home dejected from work after making a suggestion on the job about improving bus route efficiency. Norton sets up the punch line by saying something like: "Wow, that's great Ralphie boy, I bet they'll be able to cut back on bus drivers now." Ralph glares at him and answers with disgust: "*I* was the first to go."

Alice and the Blond: The Kramdens and Nortons visit the Weidemeyers, Ralph's co-worker Bert and his dizzy but very glamorous blond wife, Rita. Ralph and Ed practically trip over each other lighting Rita's cigarettes, sliding out her chair and doing anything else they can for her. Alice and Trixie believe their husbands are neglecting them, and cut the evening short, but not before some great lines got delivered. Rita is telling the group how she and Bert have pet names for each other based on some physical characteristic of theirs, and asks the wives if they do likewise. "Oh sure," Alice says brightly, turning to Ralph, "Isn't that right *Tubby*."

Thanks to Jackie Gleason, Audrey Meadows, Art Carney and Joyce Randolph for telling the stories of people who would never get their fifteen minutes of fame, but who were the heart and soul of the great place called Brooklyn.

Chapter 47: THE MAGIC OF RADIO

Anyone who grew up during the 1950s knows that radio was the pre-eminent form of entertainment for most American families. Whether it was after dinner listening to well-known family favorites like Jack Benny, or up in your room under the covers in the dark listening to scary stories on Lights Out, the radio, fueled by your imagination could take you anywhere.

When I say radio, I'm talking about a serious looking piece of furniture that dominated living rooms the way your plasma TV does today. Early radio manufacturers included Crosley, Admiral, Philco, and Zenith. My wife recently bought me a couple of CD sets of old radio shows, and listening to them was a thrill. (I thrill easily these days.) They brought back wonderful memories of some favorites from my radio days:

One of my childhood heroes was The Lone Ranger. He and Tonto always turned up wherever they were needed, never shot to kill, never waited around to be thanked, and left behind a silver bullet to remember him by. All together now, as he and Tonto ride into the sunset: "Who was that masked man?"

Adventure shows were plentiful. I liked The Green Lantern, Gene Autry, Sergeant Preston of the Yukon, and The Third Man starring Orson Welles. Welles also voiced The Shadow, whose opening line was: "Who knows what evil lurks in the hearts of Men, the Shadow." Typically these shows featured a cliff-hanging ending guaranteed to have you glued to your radio for next week's episode.

We had spooky shows too. The one that I remember best was a show called Lights Out. It began with a man saying in a deep, other-worldly voice: "L-i-i-i-ghts Out". When I think about the graphic gore in today's horror films, I smile thinking about how these two lousy words scared the crap out of me. The show later transitioned successfully to TV and scared me even worse.

Comedy shows were also popular. Jack Benny, Groucho Marx, Ozzie and Harriet, and a show that eventually became a favorite of mine when it moved to television, Amos and Andy. The show was driven off the air by pressure from African-Americans who considered the show racist. I can see their point for the radio show, which starred two white men, but the TV show had an all black cast and was less racist than some of the TV shows on today that depict blacks as horrible stereotypes.

The characters on Amos and Andy represented blacks from all walks of life in truly funny situations. The show was an example of other shows of the day that depicted ethnic families in funny situations. Some examples: Luigi Bosco (Italians); The Goldbergs (Jews). Cancellation of the show not only deprived viewers, but put a lot of black actors out of work.

It's hard to convey what radio meant to us. Kids today, with their laptops, video games and cell phones would probably find it incredibly tame. For us it was a magic carpet.

Chapter 48: PENNIES FROM HEAVEN

I sometimes wonder what it would take for a person to stoop down and pick up a coin these days. I know pennies don't stand a chance. Nickels might still have a shot, but only if nobody's looking. Dimes are small and harder to see. It's embarrassing to stoop down for what you think is a dime and then, have to pretend to be tying your shoe when you realize it's only a piece of foil. I guess I'd have to say that quarters offer the best odds of getting picked up by just about everyone. It wasn't always so.

In the Fifties even pennies had value. In Sam's Candy Store stood a case with sliding glass doors, where penny candies were displayed... marshmallow peanuts, wax lips, licorice pipes, Mary Janes, candy cigarettes, wax bottles filled with sweet liquid, Bazooka Bubble Gum, those long paper strips with rows of colored candy dots and so many others. We would stand there trying to decide how to invest our penny, while Sam watched us like a hawk. Gum ball and peanut vending machines also took pennies, and they looked very cool in "penny loafers" if you were lucky enough to own a pair.

A nickel was more of a middle-class investment. It would buy any one of fifty candy bars like Three Musketeers, Clark Bar, Baby Ruth, or Mounds...all about twice the size they are today. Five cents got you a whole pack of baseball cards that smelled like the bubble gum they were packed with. You could spring for a fountain Coke or a Lime Rickey, a Dixie Cup Ice Cream with pictures of celebrities on the inside lid. Down in the subway, before they had to be removed due to vandalism, were soda vending machines that dispensed five flavors at the push of a button. If you were lucky, the cup would drop down before the seltzer and flavored syrup came out.

John D. Rockefeller used to give shiny new dimes to kids because he knew their value in "boy currency". For a dime you got any of the dozens of colorful comic books arrayed on Sam's shelves, the ice cream of your choice from the Bungalow Bar truck, a shoe shine at my grandfather's store on Rockaway Avenue, a 3-pack of Yankee Doodles, a Mission pineapple soda ice cold from the red ice chest, a ride on the subway, or a phone call in one of those great old wooden phone booths. You could dine on a Sabrette's Hot Dog, one of Mom's Knishes hot off the cart, and for dessert, shaved ices with your choice of flavored syrups.

The most precious coin was the elusive quarter. There was a subway grating outside the Cactus Pool Room on Fulton Street. Sometimes one of the boys would accidentally drop a quarter down the grating where it beckoned from twenty feet below street level. When it was spotted, we swung into action. Somebody would borrow a padlock from home. We would shinny under a car to get a gob of axle grease to coat the bottom of the padlock. Then, after tying a length of string to the top of the padlock, we would go fishing for the quarter in the subway grate. It was hard and dirty work, but success meant candy bars for everyone.

Did we feel sorry for ourselves for being so poor that we had to resort to such tactics for a lousy candy bar? Never. We were having too much fun. We knew how to amuse ourselves without bothering an adult to entertain us. God, how I loved being a kid in 1950s Brooklyn.

Chapter 49: THE LITTLE GLASS WINDOWS

We didn't get to eat out much as kids. Money was always tight and we didn't have the variety of fast food places available today where families on a budget could get a meal without a bank loan.

One place I MENTIONED EARLIER that was affordable for us was the Horn and Hardart Automat. This was a chain of cafeteria-style restaurants where you got your food by dropping the required number of nickels in the slot and retrieving it from behind little glass windows.

There were a number of locations around including downtown Brooklyn. The promise of going there was the only way mom could get me to accompany her on shopping excursions to stores like Abraham and Strauss and Martin's. There was also one near Radio City Music Hall, that magnificent art deco theater in Manhattan where we attended the annual Christmas extravaganza featuring the fabulous Rockettes.

The fascination with the Automat for a kid was the dazzling array of food placed behind a wall of tiny windows including foods you might not ever see at home. You had maybe a dollar in nickels in your pocket, and you were master of your culinary choices.

They featured an assortment of main dishes, sandwiches, sides and desserts. My favorites were the franks and beans, mac and cheese, beef pot pie, pecan pie and homemade lemonade. They had a fountain in the shape of a silver lion that dispensed hot chocolate out of the lion's mouth.

As an Australian observer wrote a few years after the Automat opened in New York, the average man becomes a "manipulator of destiny," suddenly finding himself "before Ali Baba's cave. He whispers 'Open sesame!' and lo! a ham sandwich or a peach dumpling is his for the taking, also for a nickel."

The first Automat opened July 2, 1912, in Times Square. The last one on Third Avenue in Manhattan closed in 1991. For a kid armed with a pocketful of nickels, it was a magical place to dine.

Chapter 50: BROTHER RAYMOND

What makes our school days so memorable is that as children, we are sent to school like blank pages, ready to be filled up with the academic knowledge that will help us get along in life. This knowledge is imparted by our teachers who become like surrogate parents, each taking part in our development for one year and then handing us off to the next higher grade where the process continues. Most of us can point with gratitude to those teachers who had the most positive influence on our young lives. I had two such teachers that I remember very fondly, Brother Jude, and Patricia Hornberger. Unfortunately, we shudder as we also recall the bad teachers. Brother Raymond was one.

My old grammar school, Our Lady of Lourdes employed women teachers for grades 1 to 4; there was no Kindergarten in the dark ages. For grades 5-8 the girls were taught by nuns, the Sisters of St. Joseph, and the boys by Franciscan Brothers. In the days when physical discipline was a reality in the classroom, teachers ruled mostly by fear. This sounds harsh, but in reality it eliminated a lot of the nonsense distractions teachers have to cope with today, and if you toed the line, you were usually OK. The nuns and brothers established the rules early on and you obeyed them, end of story. If you strayed, you paid.

Brother Raymond was the most feared disciplinarian in the school. His biggest regret in life was that he had missed out on the Spanish Inquisition. Instead, he took out his frustrations on the thirteen-year old boys placed in his care. Catholicism is a basically good religion that sometimes attracts bad people like pedophile priests. Brother Raymond was one such type. Short but muscular, bald and humorless, he patrolled the hallways like a malevolent force, and as he was the 8th grade teacher, you knew you had to pass through his class before you graduated.

I remember older boys moving up from Brother Jude's 7th grade class, and how they changed when they met Brother Raymond in 8th grade. A shadow passed across their normally cheerful countenances as they prepared to spend a long year with the Angel of Death. Brother Raymond not only enjoyed physically abusing boys, but humiliating them as well. Maybe he had a Napoleonic complex and felt he had to live up to his reputation. There were also rumors of "inappropriate touching", but they were never addressed publically. We all knew he was waiting for us like a dark cloud we had to pass through. "I'll get you my pretty, and your little dog too!"

In my years at Lourdes I found there were brothers who looked fierce on the outside but always had some redeeming quality that made them approachable. Brother Raymond was pure evil. I know some day he will have to answer to a higher power for all the boys he brutalized. As I finished the 7th grade, and was steeling myself for the fate that awaited me, the sun suddenly broke through the clouds. The hated Brother Raymond was leaving the school (maybe there was something to those inappropriate touching allegations after all) and my man Brother Jude was assigned to the 8th grade.

In life we occasionally get unexpected breaks thrown our way. We may not deserve them but by the grace of God they come anyway. Thank you Lord for delivering me from clutches of Brother Raymond.

Chapter 51: BOY MEETS GIRL

It's a miracle that men and women ever get together. When interest in the opposite sex first begins during our pre-teens, there are so many obstacles to that first "date" to say nothing of a lasting relationship and eventually, marriage. Things have changed a lot since I first noticed girls. On the surface Kids seem to be way more sophisticated and confident around the opposite sex, but if you look carefully, there is that same angst experienced by every generation since the Romans. Sadly, there is no real instruction in the process. While it's true that sex education is taught in the classroom, there are no classes for social interactions between boys and girls; it's pretty much trial and error.

Typically, it is the female of the species that lights the fuse. Girls are more mature than boys in those awkward pre-teen years, and they usually lead the way with shier and socially clueless boys. When I was in seventh grade, it started. "You know, Maria likes you" one of Maria's friends would whisper to some unsuspecting boy in the schoolyard. "Huh" would come the sophisticated reply. (Seventh grade guys are more interested in sports than girls, and a little slow on the uptake.) "She _likes_ you" whispers Maria's friend a bit more urgently, usually accompanied by a punch in the arm to shake Mr. Right out of his lethargy. What Maria's friend doesn't know is that Mr. Right has no understanding what the term "likes" means in this context, and even if he did, wouldn't have any idea what to do about it.

In the 1950s, nobody talked about sex. You never even heard the word mentioned. Adolescent boys would notice their bodies changing and certain stirrings coming over them, but nobody was there to explain how normal this was. In our Catholic school the Franciscan Brothers who taught us were not the most reliable guides in this wilderness. They might obliquely refer to these feelings as temptations of the devil to be vigorously resisted by doing endless push-ups. And so each boy struggled alone, not realizing that all his classmates were navigating the same uncharted waters. It was an uncomfortable time, full of uncertainty. Through it all, girls were those mysterious creatures that inhabited the classrooms in the other half of the school building.

My earliest memories of any social contact with girls are the party games like Spin the Bottle and Post Office that were played in someone's basement. Of course the girls (like Eve at the dawning of time) took the lead in organizing these recreations. There was always another room to which the boy and girl singled out to kiss would adjourn, accompanied by the hoots and jeers of their friends. At first the guys were mortified by these activities, but soon learned to happily join in. Suddenly, Moms were finding lipstick on collars, and the race was on. Guys and gals began pairing off and spending time together. Hand-holding in public (never within a mile of school), going to movies, and sharing an ice cream soda at the neighborhood were typical behaviors.

The next step in this drama was called "going steady". Sometimes this new phase of the relationship was cemented with an inexpensive ring or school sweater, but more often than not, it just became understood. Going steady meant you couldn't date other people and that you were off the market for all intents and purposes. Games of Spin the Bottle were rigged so that couples who were going steady always got each other as partners. Some of these tween romances lasted right up to the altar, but usually the road to finding a life partner was littered with a few broken hearts. The increasingly high divorce rate speaks to the fact that lasting compatibility between women and men is elusive...a minefield filled with hazards that can tank any romance.

As a society we need to do more to help boys and girls ease into social relationships. Despite the odds, some of us are lucky enough to find that person who completes us; for this we are most grateful.

As you can see, I was extremely lucky in love. My wife, Jasmine.

Chapter 52: GO FLY A KITE

The cost of amusing kids has gone through the roof. Most are now into electronic or video games that run around forty bucks on average to buy, not to mention the "box" these games are played on. The cost is not measured in money alone; the real price we pay for kids' addiction to these games is that they rarely play outdoors any more. They become isolated from social interaction with other kids and spend way too many hours playing these games, the worst of which are violent and can desensitize a child to unacceptable behavior. Other games draw kids into fantasy adventures to the point where they develop unhealthy obsessions and blur the line between make-believe and reality.

Fifties kids in Brooklyn never saw forty dollar toys. Sure we had fantasy heroes like Flash Gordon and The Lone Ranger, but when play time was over, we hung up our ray guns and cowboy hats and played baseball, football, punch ball, stick ball and stoop ball. On any given day, we could entertain ourselves for under twenty-five cents.

Pea shooters, spinning tops, yo-yos, pitching pennies...all activities that fell within this modest budget. One of my favorite 25-cent toys was a paper kite. We would buy them in Sam's or Louie's candy store for fifteen cents, and add two rolls of string for a nickel each. No kid would settle for flying his kite only as high as one roll would allow; we tied two rolls together to really get that baby up there.

The kites were brightly colored and came rolled around two balsa-wood sticks that needed to be assembled to form the cross-shaped frame of the kite. It took a bit of skill to get the kite together without tearing it. We learned little tricks to keep the kite from breaking apart while being buffeted by the winds at higher altitudes.

One such trick was to tie the sticks that formed the frame together with a short piece of string at the point where they crossed. This strengthened the kite and gave it greater stability when aloft. We also experimented with different types of kite tails, an essential addition for ease of flying. Many a mother never learned that her missing pillow case had been torn into strips and was dangling at the end of a kite.

We preferred to fly our kites in places like Highland Park where there were no electrical wires to complicate safe landings. There were also different ways to rig the kite so that it could perform aerial maneuvers. Sometimes we would let two competing kites battle it out in the sky. One enterprising kid tried the James Bond-like trick of tying his fathers old double-edged razor blades to his kite's tail in the hope that it would shred his opponent's kite. (He probably grew up to work in government.) His shabby tactics backfired when he sustained a bad cut after absentmindedly grabbing his kite by the tail as he reeled it in for a landing.

And so for a measly quarter, we got practice assembling things with our hands, learned kite-building innovations (no matter how despicable) that would give us a competitive edge, and got all the fresh air and exercise we could stand. Take that, Nintendo.

Chapter 53: THINGS ITALIAN MOTHERS SAY

Back in the Fifties, before an Italian woman was permitted to become a mother, she was required to attend Marie Barrone Boot Camp and memorize a set of sayings that she would use to guide the development of her children for the rest of her life. Every kid raised in an Italian home heard these sayings at some time growing up. It wasn't just the words...they had to be said in a special way so that they bored right through your thin outer layer of bravado and struck you deep in that guilt-ridden place in your heart. It didn't matter either if you were five or fifty, living at home or on your own, you were always fair game. Here are some of my favorites.

Finish your dinner...kids in Europe are starving.

Now I was a pretty good eater so I didn't hear this one that much, but there were certain foods I just would not touch. Boiled fish, lamb, lima beans, cabbage, Brussels sprouts, asparagus, anything that looked slimy. I would push them around my plate or try to hide them, and when Mom reminded me about the starving children I wanted to say: "Here's an idea, why not just wrap up those sprouts and mail them back to Brussels". I knew that if I ever wised-off like this it would bring a sharp rap to the head with the dreaded wooden spoon, so I just shut up. I always wondered if there was some kind of bizarre guilt-exchange deal made whereby European mothers used starving children in America to get kids to eat their pierogis.

If (insert name here) jumped off the Brooklyn Bridge would you do it too?

This one came out when you wanted to do something your mother opposed, and you set her up by foolishly saying: "Well Vinnie gets to do it". (Buzzer sound, Sorry, wrong answer but we have some lovely parting gifts for you. Thanks for playing.) And then Mom says, wait for it now, "If Vinnie jumped off the Brooklyn Bridge, would you do it too?" I don't think it ever occurred to Vinnie to jump off any bridge, and if he was crazy enough to try it, I certainly wouldn't follow. There was no kid comeback however that would counter this bridge argument. The Mother's Handbook said that this saying, when uttered with sarcastic contempt, would quell any foolish thing your child wanted to do, and by God it did.

Wait till your father gets home.

This was the Italian mother's last resort after she had tried every trick she knew to get you to stop behaving like a jerk. Mothers were smart enough to use it sparingly to avoid diluting the ominous threat these words carried. When you had pushed your poor mother to the brink she took a deep breath and let it fly. The words were spoken slowly and deliberately, as if blows were being delivered. *"Wait (smack) until (smack) your (smack) father (smack) gets (smack) home."* I always felt bad for my father. He wasn't mad at me, and usually too tired from work to chase me around the kitchen table, but he had to make an effort. If Dad hit me I tried hard to pretend it really hurt because I knew his performance in carrying out my sentence was being judged by Mom, and God help him if I didn't suffer.

I only pray that someday you have a kid like you.

This was my introduction to the concept of Karma...what goes around comes around. The Italians probably have a more sinister term for it since we have sinister terms for *everything*. I thought at the time that they needed to pull this one out of the Mothers Handbook because it had absolutely no effect on me. I wanted to say: "That's it? That's all you got? That someday if I get married I might have a kid like me? I'll take my chances". Little did I know that this was an Italian "time-release" curse that always came true...genetics guarantees it. I'm extremely proud of my children, but there were times when they were growing up that my mother's words came back to haunt me.

I'm not mad at you, just disappointed.

Bullseye. This was the dum-dum bullet that mothers loaded in the guilt gun when regular bullets were not having the desired effect. They usually played this card when you were too old to hit, and smart enough to realize that the impact of these words hurt more than any hairbrush across your butt. I could withstand any corporal punishment my parents could dish out, but no kid wanted to be a disappointment to his *mother*. The phrase stopped you in your tracks, and no matter how argumentative you were feeling, you usually stared down at your shoes and mumbled something like: "Aw I'm sorry Mom, please forgive me". Score one for mamma. Hey, even Superman feared Kryptonite.

Mother's Day is coming up and it makes me think about how I could have been a better son. There are small and big things I would do differently if I had the chance, but there are no do-overs in life. I am the son of an Italian mother, and any good in me comes mostly from her. While it may be true that I could have been a better son, she could not have been a better mother.

My mother Frances, from whom any good in me comes

Chapter 54: SNOWBOUND

The blizzard of 2010…what a storm it was. New York City was totally unprepared for this and made the poorest response to a snow storm since Mayor John Lindsay back in 1969. Then, as now, the City's outer boroughs were forgotten while glitzy Manhattan, home to the fat cats, was handled as a priority. As I sit at the window watching my fellow Staten Islanders try to deal with 29 inches of un-plowed snow, my mind drifts back to the days when I actually liked the stuff. From the ages of 5 to 12, I enjoyed snow about as much as any city kid possibly could. The very things that annoy me about it now as an adult are what made it so appealing to me back then as a kid.

First, schools would close. That was in the day when mothers were mostly home caring for their families and not working like so many have to these days. Today, desperate parents show up at the school door expecting their kids to be admitted no matter the conditions. NYC schools almost never close any more, and when they do, people are outraged. In the 50's common sense prevailed. Why risk teacher and student safety when it was just simpler to have everyone stay home. The State allowed adequate snow days so why not use them. If there was no other reason to love snow as a kid, not having to go to school would have been enough.

Then there was the luxury of playing in the streets. Normally crowded with traffic, playing on a Brooklyn street could be hazardous to your health. Not that we didn't manage; we played stickball between cars, and if a play was in progress we just called time until the cars passed. City kids learn early to adapt. When it snowed it was a different story. Everything was white and quiet. Old fashioned wooden sleds with metal runners came out of the cellars and soon the streets were filled with kids belly-flopping down the block. We would "chain" the sleds together by having each kid hold onto the feet of the kid on the sled in front of him, and this sled train would go careening down the hill of the vacant lot right across the street since there were no cars to impede our progress.

Snow forts and snowball fights were mandatory. Our mothers were not used to having bored kids underfoot, and so they bundled us up in snow suits and sent us out into the drifts to play. Most homeowners shoveled their sidewalks and piled the snow near the curb, unlike the idiots today who throw it into the streets. These piles of snow became the rudimentary beginnings of elaborate snow forts, as they were added to by swarming boys eager to finish their fort before their enemies across the street could finish theirs. Towers were added, then ledges on which snowballs could be stored in preparation for an all-out attack. Small windows were poked into the walls so that the movements of the enemy could be observed.

When all was ready, war was declared. The rules of war were simple: no rocks packed inside snow balls, and no attacks if time was called due to injury. We were civilized after all. At first it was an artillery battle with each side lofting snowballs toward the enemy camp in hopes of hitting a random head that chose to peek at the wrong time. At some point, when one side sensed an advantage, an all-out assault was mounted. Garbage can covers provided excellent shields for the attacking forces as they overran the enemy position, pelting combatants with snowballs they carried in their pockets or just stopped and made on the spot. A successful raid ended by kicking down the other side's fort and burying them in their own defenses.

As violent and heated as these wars might sound, it was just play. It wasn't uncommon after the hostilities for both sides to join forces and build a snow tunnel along the sidewalk mounds, or line both sides of the street and hurl snowballs at any car that dared to drive down our block. Sometimes we had to rush home to change out of soaking wet snow suits and into dry ones. Our mothers, anxious to be rid of us, performed this maneuver like an Indy pit crew anxious to get their driver back out on the track. At the end of the day, exhausted but happy, we dragged ourselves home, put our wet gloves and hats on the radiator in the hall, and collapsed. If it was a good day, a mug of cocoa and steaming bowl of Campbell's Chicken Noodle Soup, salty enough to kill a horse, was waiting. Sublime.

I guess it's possible to use up one's supply of enthusiasm for anything. Maybe I hate snow so much today because of the intensity with which I loved it as a boy.

Chapter 55: COFFEE AND CAKE

The days when nearly all our relatives lived within walking distance are long gone. Growing up in Brooklyn, virtually three generations of our family lived in a one mile circle around the intersection of Rockaway Avenue and Fulton Street. The only ones who did not were my father's brother Joe and his family and the family members still living in Grassano in southern Italy, with whom, sadly, we maintained no contact. My son was able to track down long lost relatives on Facebook, but it's a tenuous process at best. The Italian branch goes by the name of "Pantaleo" as it appeared on their immigration records. Somehow in passing through Ellis Island, the name got changed to "Pantaleno" which is how we are known today. When I tracked down those immigration records, it was a shock to say the least to find out that indeed we have been living under a different name than our ancestors.

That one-mile circle in Brooklyn was pretty much our world. We saw our extended family frequently at holidays, birthday parties, weddings, christenings and funerals. We thought nothing of living in close proximity to each other; that's how everybody in the neighborhood lived. In between events we just dropped over for coffee and cake, a dying custom by the way now that everybody shudders at the mere mention of cake. We played outside with our cousins, literally growing up together. Clothes and toys were passed around until they wore out. If anybody was going through a tough patch, the family was there for support. People looked out for each other, and not just family members. The "mothers' miracle network" knew pretty much everything, and if you did something wrong, the news reached your Mom even before you got home.

And then all that began to change as Brooklyn changed. We were used to having people in the neighborhood who looked like us. As Blacks and Hispanics moved in, whites panicked and fled to the suburbs. My Aunt Mary moved to Selden, Long Island, a wilderness in the late fifties. My Aunt Anna moved to the edges of Brooklyn bordering Queens. Even my parents moved to Ozone Park, but not before our home in Brooklyn had lost nearly all its value. My Dad had maybe the worst instincts for real estate decisions ever; his motto might as well have been: "Buy High, Sell Low." The conveniences we were so used to having, like stores, schools, churches and great public transportation within walking distance were gone. Funny, I recently heard through a mutual acquaintance from a Trappist Monk named Father Augustine who was born on the same block as me, but is now stationed in Tennessee. He says one of the things he misses most is good Italian bread, apparently unknown in Tennessee.

Through the 1960s, our family continued to spread out, moving to far-flung places like Arizona, North Carolina, Florida, Maryland, and New Jersey. We had a fairly large contingent in Long Island. Things were just not the same. We saw each other pretty much only at weddings and wakes. Cousins and their children grew up without ever seeing much of their extended family. We had a family reunion a few years back and it was a wonderful sight to see first and second cousins getting to know each other as if they were strangers, which in essence they were.

I know things can never be the same for them, but I remember how it was for me growing up in Brooklyn surrounded by family, and I can't help being a little sad for my children and grandchildren that they will never know that feeling.

My mother's sister Anna and her family. From left, Frank, Cathy, Anna, Jim, Anna Marie, Pat

Mom's other sister, Mary, with her first born, Millie.

Chapter 56: THE HALLS OF MONTEZUMA

The "Marine Hymn" is the official hymn of the United States Marine Corps and the oldest fight song in the U.S. military. The opening bars of the hymn include the phrase: 'Halls of Montezuma', which refers to the Battle of Chapultepec during the Mexican-American War, where a force of Marines stormed Chapultepec Castle. Why the history lesson? Well as a kid, the phrase had a different meaning for me because of my Brooklyn frame of reference. I remember thinking that wherever Montezuma was, it must have been one hell of an apartment building if they wrote an entire song just about the halls.

Apartment buildings dotted Brooklyn neighborhoods like our own little Chapultepec Castles. They were interspersed with residential row houses, now called by the fancier term 'brownstones' since real estate prices went up. These 4-6 story structures ranged from funky functional to surprisingly elegant, and housed the huddled masses that flocked to places like Brooklyn during the immigration wave of the early twentieth century. Each building had several apartments on a floor, and tenants in adjoining units got to know each other a lot better than they cared to. The lobbies always smelled of cabbage, a testament to the culinary tastes of the residents.

Hallways of apartment buildings were used for a surprising number of activities. On rainy days there was usually a bunch of kids sitting on the marble entrance steps playing Briscola, a card game imported from Italy. We learned some of the finer points of the game from the old Italian men who played on the park benches on sunny days, like how to silently communicate with your partner. This was a form of cheating to be sure, but a vital advantage in a game where knowing your partner's hand gave you a decided advantage. Sometimes the older neighborhood guys would get up a crap game under the stairs that let to the basement. If the games got loud or vulgar, the building super would usually chase us out into the street.

Many a Brooklyn kid had his first cigarette in the back hallway of an apartment building. We didn't dare risk being seen smoking in the street since we knew the neighborhood women would send silent messages on their 'jungle drums' over the rooftops and back to our parents, and we would pay dearly for our folly. We would snitch unfiltered cigarettes like Luckies, Chesterfields or Camels from the packs in our fathers' pockets and light up like big shots. Those were the days when smoking was in vogue, and 'inhaling' was a rite of passage. Incredibly, actors, sports figures, and even *doctors* promoted the relaxing benefits of cigarettes.

Another more romantic activity was stealing your first kiss. If you lived in a private row house, there was always a watchful parent at the window, waiting for you, a worthless hoodlum in their eyes, to bring their daughters home from a date. This was definitely a mood killer. If you were lucky enough to be dating a girl who lived in an apartment building, you had more leeway since the entrance wasn't always visible from her apartment. You planned your move carefully, always carrying a pack of Juicy Fruit gum to cover up the smell of Chesterfields on your breath. At the right moment you moved in, trying to anticipate which way she might angle her head to avoid the awkward 'nose bump'. You also prayed that some nosy neighbor wouldn't be taking the dog for a walk during your big 'Tyrone Power' moment.

Over the years, New York City took the idea of the apartment building in a horribly wrong direction when it started constructing 'housing projects', huge complexes with hundreds of dwelling units. Adopting the 'bigger is better' theory, they moved from small buildings where everybody knew and looked out for their neighbors to over sized, impersonal brick monstrosities that became breeding grounds for crime and helped to doom so many city neighborhoods.

(By the way, I must confess that I didn't really think that the Halls of Montezuma were in an apartment building, but it did provide a nifty title for this essay.)

Chapter 57:   THE DREAM GLOVE

When you're poor, sometimes even relatively simple things seem almost unattainable. This is especially true for kids. Don't get me wrong, as a kid I didn't mope around feeling sorry for myself, but instinctively you felt that if something cost more than you could ever save up, it wasn't meant to be. Looking back, there were times when that pattern was broken...those magical moments when the planets and stars aligned, and suddenly the unattainable was yours. When these treasures came into your possession, it made a real impression, more so than for those who take them for granted. Here is a special one that I remember most fondly.

As a baseball player, you made the occasional splash with a big hit...maybe drove in the winning run late in the game, but you made your reputation with your glove. A good defensive player was greatly valued by coaches and never sat on the bench. As an outfielder I was solid defensively for my grammar school and high school teams. I had a strong arm, got a good jump on fly balls off the bat, and I was fast enough to run them down. Unfortunately the glove I used was a badly worn hand-me-down. The pocket was too small for an outfielder, not like the newer model gloves that were in the windows of the Davega sporting goods store on Pitkin Avenue in Brooklyn.

Davega's sold uniforms and equipment for most sports, and its windows were a powerful lure for kids. We would stare at the magnificent array of satin team jackets, colorful uniforms, footballs, basketballs, hockey sticks, and especially the baseball gloves. Gloves for infielders, first baseman's mitts with those two big fingers, catcher's mitts with perfectly padded pockets for handling blazing fastballs, and there, on a plastic display stand, was the glove I craved with all my being, the Rawlings Don Larsen model glove. It was a thing of beauty, all soft, buttery leather and rawhide stitching, with the red Rawlings label on the outside. It was huge, made for leaping, acrobatic catches that turned sure home runs into routine outs. I could almost feel my teammates pounding me on the back as I trotted back to our bench...great catch Jim, and coach Bryan muttering: Good 'D' kid!

Who was I kidding, the glove cost around sixty bucks, serious money in the Fifties. I wanted to go into the store to ask the man if I could try it on, you know, just to see how it felt. I changed my mind when I realized how much worse I would feel if I actually touched the glove, smelled its pungent leather, and pounded the pocket with my fist. I decided against it, and made up my mind not to look in that store window so much because the sheer *longing* for that glove was making me crazy. I'd do the best I could with my old glove and the hell with it.

That Christmas I was excited since even poor kids get stuff under the tree. As my sister and I opened gifts, I spotted a box shaped like it contained a pair of shoes. (Hey, it may have been Christmas, but it wasn't uncommon for parents to slip in a few practical things you needed anyhow in the guise of a present.) As I took off the paper, my eyes widened and my jaw dropped. There it was, nestled in red tissue paper, my Rawlings Don Larsen model outfielder's glove! I couldn't speak. If the box had contained a million dollars in cash I couldn't have been more surprised. I saw the smile on my father's face...I can only imagine how hard he must have worked to persuade my mother to make such an extravagant purchase.

It was months until baseball season but that glove never left my sight. I rubbed it with linseed oil and, after placing a baseball in the pocket to help shape it, wrapped it with rubber bands until it was molded to the perfect fit. I used that glove until the leather was nearly worn away, and I'll say with some modesty that over the years I took my share of extra base hits away from disappointed hitters. We tried not to spoil our kids as they grew up, but sometimes, when you knew how badly they wanted something that cost a lot of money, you caved in and bought it. Seeing the looks on their faces was worth it.

I just hope my Dad got his sixty bucks worth from the look on my face that Christmas morning so long ago. I still keep it in his memory.

My grammar school team: Our Lady of Lourdes, circa 1956

Still have my Rawlings dream glove

Chapter 58: SIBLING SALUTE

I've written here about my parents, my block in Brooklyn, my schools, some neighborhood characters and places, even holidays and how we celebrated them in our family. One topic I haven't reminisced about is my younger siblings, Cathy, my sister and Anthony, my brother.

Cathy is about two years younger than i. We share a lot of childhood memories since we are fairly close in age. We got along reasonably well for sister and brother; I'm sure there were times I teased her, but she is too good-natured to hold it against me. Cathy attended the same school as I, Our Lady of Lourdes, only we didn't see each other that much since she sat on the girls' side of the building while I sat with the boys. Back then she palled around with three other girls her age who all lived within a few houses of each other. There was Pamela, Loretta, and Phyllis, and when you saw one, the others were usually nearby. I remember her jumping rope with her friends and chanting the ditties girls used to keep time while jumping: " 'A' my name is Anna and my husband's name is Al, we come from Alabama and we sell apples".

Cathy was a pretty, popular kid, and also an excellent student. She loved to laugh and to this day has a smile that can make your day. She graduated from William Maxwell Vocational High School and went on to a successful career as an executive secretary with J.P. Morgan. In those days secretaries took dictation in shorthand and typed on manual typewriters as big as Buicks. When Cathy started her career, secretaries were invaluable to key executives; there are very few real secretaries around today since everyone types their own e-mails and answers their own phones. My sister is a thoughtful, caring person who always sends *exactly* the right greeting card for every occasion.

My brother Anthony came along later. He is 11 years younger than I, and the baby of the family. Being so much older, I didn't spend much time with my brother growing up. By the time he was only seven years old, I was already in the Army. Around then my parents moved from East New York to the wilds of Richmond Hill in Queens, so his childhood in the suburbs was different from mine. Anthony is the musician in the family, playing guitar to this day. He is a devoted Beatles fan and still attends the annual vigil of John Lennon's birthday held on October 9th every year in the area of Central Park designated as Strawberry Fields. Married to Doctor Michele Seitz in St. Patrick's Cathedral, they live in Lynbrook, NY with their three beautiful daughters, Elizabeth, Margaret and Kaitlyn.

Tony graduated from my old High School, Brooklyn Tech, but by this time it just becoming co-ed, again, a very different experience from mine. He graduated from Queens College, got a Masters in School Psychology from Pace University, and a Doctorate in the same discipline from Fordham University. He is the resident school psychologist at John Glenn High School in East Northport, N.Y. and has a private practice specializing in helping troubled teens. Dr. Pantaleno was named 2007 NYS School Psychologist of the Year by the New York State Association of School Psychologists and the 2008 Psychologist of the Year by the Suffolk County Psychological Association. I am very proud of my brother's professional accomplishments, but prouder still of his being a good husband, father and brother.

I'm glad I wasn't an only child. Having a sister and a brother was good in a lot of ways, not the least of which was having other kids in the house to distract my parents' attention. It's hard to believe so many years have passed since we were kids.

My sister Cathy making her First Communion

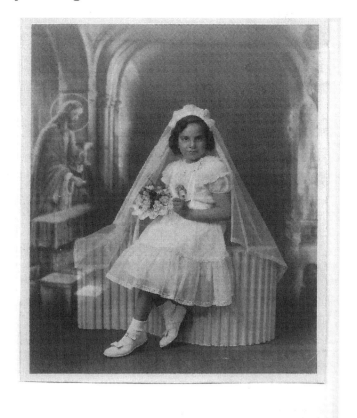

Brother Tony on guitar

Chapter 59:   TECH ALMA MATER

The title of this piece comes from the opening words to the Brooklyn Technical H.S. Alma Mater song as we sang it when I attended from 1956 to 1960. The school was all boys back then; they have since changed the words of the song to reflect the molding of women as well. "Tech" as we called it was known as one of the best high schools in New York City, along with Stuyvesant H.S. and the Bronx H.S. of Science. For me, going to high school was a tough transition. Having attended a small parochial grammar school where I spent eight years with pretty much the same forty kids, going to a new school that housed *6,000* boys was an adjustment to say the least.

The school building was enormous. Located in downtown Brooklyn, the yellow brick monolith housed not only classrooms, but specialized labs, sheet-metal, machine and wood shops, a foundry, an operating radio station, basement pool and rooftop gym. In case you're wondering why a foundry in a NYC high school, Tech prided itself on preparing students for not just college, but careers in technical fields such as Chemistry, Architecture, Aeronautics, Electronics and Mechanical Drawing. The foundry was where we poured molten metal into a sand mold to create a casting of the "stepped V block" we made in wood shop. (To this day, I have no idea what a stepped V block is.)

During the years I attended Tech, William Pabst was its principal. He ran a tight ship for a public school, and nonsense was not tolerated. He had his S.O.S. (Safety, Order, Service) student patrols roaming the halls, waiting to ambush late arrivals or rat out anyone in the halls without a pass. The cafeteria had to serve lunch in shifts to accommodate the mass of students. They featured a daily "special"...a hot lunch for around 15 cents. You were also required to buy a plastic token that you would exchange for eating utensils. You would stand in line at the utensil booth, give the lady in the hairnet your token, and she would give you eating utensils for the meal. When you were done, you turned the silverware in and got your token back. They did this to prevent students from stealing the utensils or just throwing them away.

Tech had its share of fine teachers, but it harbored a few loonies too. A Mechanical Drawing teacher named Mr. Elwin would leave the room and then sneak back in, crouching beneath the desks and then *leap up* trying to catch students doing something wrong. I also had a Geometry teacher (best not to name him) who ruined math for me. He was a heavy drinker and could barely stand up much less explain plane geometry. I also seem to recall a wood shop teacher with a missing finger. (Insert your own joke here.)

The teacher who had a major influence on me taught English, and went by the name of Patricia Hornberger. I always liked reading and writing well enough, but somehow she put my love of words into another gear. Maybe because she was younger than most teachers at the school, or because she had a sense of humor and knew how to make learning *fun*. She would make us read Shakespearean plays aloud, with each student taking a turn. If you don't think it's funny listening to kids from the streets of Brooklyn read lines like: "Fly, fly, my lord! There is no tarrying here" from Julius Caesar, then think again. I can only thank providence for sending Ms. Hornburger to me. I only wish I could tell her how much her passion for teaching changed my life.

All in all, I got a good education at Tech, but because I was a bit of a jerk, never graduated and had to finish high school elsewhere. In my senior year, I got in with some bad company and was soon cutting classes regularly. Because I was able to duplicate my mother's handwriting perfectly, I wrote absence notes that were accepted by the school without question. Once I misspelled a word on one of my fake absence notes. Catching the error, I wrote a replacement note, and tucked the incorrect one into one of my books. Unfortunately it fell out, was found by another student and turned in to the school office where they saw an almost identical note already on file. After bringing my mother in for questioning, the jig was up and I was asked to leave the school. My forgery career came to an abrupt end.

Some months later, during a nocturnal trip to Rockaway Beach where we went to drink Thunderbird wine, I angrily took off my Brooklyn Tech senior ring and flung it into the ocean. (I'm a very dramatic drunk.) Not graduating Tech is one of my regrets in life. Thankfully the seeds of learning were already planted by good teachers like Patricia Hornberger, and I went on to get my Masters Degree after I matured a bit and found a partner in life who kept me on the straight and narrow.

I played varsity ball for Brooklyn Tech. Check out those classy uniforms

Chapter 60:   FRIENDS

The other day I was glancing through my grammar school graduation album, the one with the multi-colored pages that your friends wrote witty sayings in like "2 good 2 be 4 gotten" and "Remember A, Remember B, but most of all, remember me". A mixture of fun and melancholy came over me as I flipped through the pages. I smiled at the silly things my buddies wrote, and despite the slippage in my memory for things current, the faces of each boy immediately came into clear focus as I read what they wrote; I can picture them exactly as they looked over 60 years ago. Well-wishes from my parents and family members, including a page of squiggly lines from my two-year old brother, flood my brain with memories. I read touching notes from teachers, whose impact on my life I would never realize until years later.

At the time, I was close to a lot of my classmates, having spent eight years with them at Our Lady of Lourdes. We also played on the same school teams and many of them lived in my neighborhood. As I read their names and look at their faces, I realize that virtually all of them, with few exceptions, are no longer in my life. The Fifties was kind of the beginning of the great migration out of the old neighborhoods and into the suburbs. Up until then people were much more inclined to live out their lives not far from where their parents grew up. Growing up back then, you were far more likely to run into those with whom you went to school...whether at church, in the supermarket, or on the subway platform. As people moved away from their childhood residences, all that changed. People you thought were friends no longer kept in touch; the few you took the trouble to remain close to, despite being physically apart, were your real *friends*.

If we're lucky, we make a few close friends in our lifetime. There are many impediments to continuing relationships begun in childhood. Besides moving away from the neighborhood, there is the spouse issue. Sometimes friends drift apart when their spouses can't get along. People whose views in adulthood about politics or religion are markedly different find it hard to see past these differences and gradually lose contact. Sometimes gender gets in the way. Men tend to be good friends with other men and women with women. There is no earthly reason that should be the case, but there it is. I certainly count my wife as my best friend because although she knows my faults better than anyone, she still chooses to be my friend, and that means the world to me.

My two other closest friends, Rich and Phil, I have known since first grade. Considering we are all reaching the 70 and over club, that is a long time. I can't remember my life without these two special people in it. Our families were close growing up and we all hung out together. Phil became a Franciscan Brother as a young man, and then left the order to marry and have a family. Rich introduced me to my wife and we were best men at each other's weddings; Godfathers to each other's children. In our adult years we have lived in different places, Rich in Florida, Phil in Arizona and me in New York, but there has been unbroken communication by phone and e-mail all those years in addition to periodic get-togethers. When we talk, it is as if we spoke yesterday. I think of these guys as brothers who would do anything for me if I asked.

Friendship should not be confused with acquaintance. I have made many friends over the years at work and in my social life. I have genuine affection for these people and I hope they have for me, but it is not the same. I am basically a gregarious person who enjoys meeting new people. Sometimes when you meet someone, there is an immediate connection. On the Internet a few years ago I met Joe, a guy who grew up around the corner from me in my old neighborhood, and went to the same school. Joe moved with his family in the exodus to the suburbs so we never actually met as kids, but because of his East New York - Brooklyn DNA, and the fact that he grew up in similar circumstances as me, I feel as though I have known Joe all my life and consider him a friend.

Friendship is hard to define. It's not about how long you know someone, but more I think about how you both see the world. While it might be possible to form lasting friendships with those whose ideas are diametrically opposed to yours, I think too much work would be required to sustain such a relationship. I found a quote by author Richard Bach (Jonathan Livingston Seagull) that sums up friendship well enough for me:

"Your friends will know you better in the first minute you meet than your acquaintances will know you in a thousand years."

Phil, Me and Rich at Claire and Marc Simeone wedding

Our wedding, standing from left, Joe, Lefty, Phil, Rich, Tommy, Joe

Chapter 61: IS THAT MEATBALLS I SMELL

I think I was probably sixteen years old before I figured out that not everybody awoke on Sunday mornings to the smell of frying meatballs. If you were Italian and living in Brooklyn, Sunday was "gravy" day. For non-Italians, gravy is not the brown stuff you put on your turkey, but the rich, red gravy made from fresh tomatoes, tomato puree, and spices, bubbling on the stove and filled with meatballs, sausages, braccioles, and pork.

The wonderful scene from the movie "Fatso" showing Dom DeLuise dipping the heel of a loaf of Italian bread in gravy and Parmesan cheese while his poor cousin Sal lay in repose in the living room lovingly portrays just how comforting gravy can be to Italians. With all due respect (as the wiseguys say) no cuisine anywhere can compare to Italy's, period. We thought cholesterol was what they put in swimming pools to keep the water clean. Our celebrations for holidays, birthdays, baptisms, Communions, Confirmations and any other reason we could think of revolved around eating and drinking wine, as they do to this day.

An Italian holiday meal typically consisted of soup, antipasto, and maybe a lasagna or manicotti with all the aforementioned meats on the side. (Full yet?) Then came a turkey or a pot roast with all the trimmings. We would take a break, like a boxer between rounds, while fruit, roasted chestnuts, and assorted nuts were served. Then, after regaining consciousness, we would tuck into dessert which might include Italian pastry, cheesecake, pignoli cookies, blackout cake from Ebinger's Bakery and assorted homemade pies. After a pause to play poker for pennies, the chocolates and liqueurs would come out. Even had it been invented back then, Lipitor wouldn't have stood a chance.

There were no supermarkets in an Italian neighborhood. There were bakeries, salumerias, fish stores and fruit stores. The man behind the counter knew you by name, and added up your purchases with a pencil on the side of a brown paper bag. Our extended family was concentrated in a small area of Brooklyn. We saw our aunts, uncles and cousins all the time. When my Aunt Mary moved to Suffolk County, Long Island in the early sixties, it was like she moved to *Australia*. How would we get there? Did we need passports? Cars were scarce; when we did go, we usually piled into one car...every adult lap held an excited cousin looking out the windows on the wonders of the Belt Parkway. We looked like that circus car full of clowns.

Growing up I never thought of my childhood as remarkable, in fact it seemed quite ordinary to me. We played the games kids had always played, visited Coney Island, relished a trip to the Horn and Hardart Automat, and spent a lot of time with our families and extended families. We got through school, found a job, got married and had kids...that was the template for life and we pretty much followed it. Off in the future were lurking such issues as the struggles for women's equality, equal rights for minorities, gay rights, scandals in the Catholic church, the omnipresent welfare state, Woodstock, civil disobedience, Viet Nam and Islamic fundamentalist terrorism. In light of how uncomplicated my childhood seems in the rear-view mirror, I have decided in many ways that it was remarkable and one I almost wish I could guarantee for my children's children.

The old neighborhoods are changed now, but any kid who grew up Italian in Brooklyn will tell you they wouldn't have it any other way. My uncle Nick used to say that there are two kinds of people, Italians and those who wish they were. A little chauvinistic maybe, but Italians believe it in their hearts.

My big, crazy Italian family celebrating our 50th wedding anniversary

Chapter 62: FOURTH OF JULY WITH FAT SALLY

As the Fourth of July approaches these days, people prepared to attend spectacular fireworks displays sponsored by such business giants as Macy's or the local town government. These shows are carried out by professional pyrotechnists like the Grucci family of New York, a five-generation, family-owned and operated company on Long Island New York who give 300 elaborately programmed, computer-aided fireworks performances annually all around the world. It wasn't always so. Back in 1950s Brooklyn, fireworks for the Fourth were more of a hands-on affair or, if you'll forgive the pun, hands off if you were careless.

The excitement started mounting maybe in mid-June when that first cherry bomb detonation on the block signaled the arrival of a new illegal fireworks season. I was never quite sure where the fireworks came from, but there were "guys" who, year in and year out could be relied upon to sell fireworks out of their hallway or car trunk. All we knew was that they drove "down south" where fireworks were (and still are) legal, bought a supply of the most popular stuff, and then resold it at a profit in the neighborhood. This was Capitalism pure and simple. The transactions were very clandestine, although back then the cops were a lot more tolerant than today, after all, they were kids once too.

My friends and I would take the wrinkled dollar bills we had saved up and search out the shady characters who peddled this stuff. Once you told them who sent you, like in the old speakeasy days, you were accepted. No thought was given by these bums about the dangers of selling explosives to underage customers. If you had the cash, out came the stash. Cherry bombs, ash cans or M-80s, Roman candles, bottle rockets, pinwheels, firecrackers in packs of twenty and, for the feint of heart, ladyfingers and sparklers. When the big day came, we usually waited until dark to set off our explosions. We didn't just blow them up at random either; they were too expensive to squander. No, we staged elaborate scenes for maximum effect.

Maybe an ashcan (equivalent to about one-quarter stick of dynamite) would be inserted into a ripe watermelon stolen off Steve's horse-drawn cart. (Steve was a junk man in winter and changed hats to sell day-old produce at bargain prices in summer. I doubt he ever hosed out the wagon between career changes.) Sometimes we would roll cherry bombs under cars and run like hell when the owners gave chase. Every year one of us, with no hope of ever becoming a Mensa member, would man-up and hold something dangerous in his hand until the fuse had almost burned down to the powder. Amazingly, no one was ever seriously hurt, although once, during a Roman Candle fight, "Fankie"'s hair caught on fire. We called him Fankie because although his name was Frankie, he couldn't pronounce his Rs. One instant nickname, coming up.

Fireworks were a common way to celebrate Independence Day in most New York City neighborhoods. The cops had murderers to catch and weren't very interested in busting kids for illegal fireworks, as long as you kept it *sane*. At some point that last proviso was forgotten, but it wasn't us kids who screwed it up, but Neanderthal adults. They would light a fire in a big, cast iron garbage pail out in the street and just sit there lobbing in all sorts of fireworks, hour after hour. Some of these would be blown out of the pail and explode on someone's stoop or front yard. The poster boy for dangerous, over-the-top fireworks displays was John Gotti. Every year the Teflon Don would sponsor such an event in the Howard Beach community. At first the cops left it alone, but as Gotti became more notorious, they shut him down on Mayor Rudy Giuliani's orders.

For me fireworks on the Fourth of July were a part of growing up . They are less commonly seen in New York City neighborhoods these days because of a zero-tolerance crackdown by police. I guess that makes some sense, but I'm glad for the thrills we got from setting off fireworks as kids. To us it was mostly harmless fun (Brooklyn style) and I'm happy to report all fingers and toes are intact.

Chapter 63:   WHO NEEDS RODEO DRIVE

Rodeo Drive, the renowned shopping mecca in Beverly Hills has nothing on Brooklyn's Pitkin Avenue in the 1950s. Between Rockaway and Saratoga Avenues along Pitkin stood retail shops, restaurants and theaters...it was the place to shop, eat and be entertained. I remember lots of shoe stores like Thom McCan, Florshiem, and A.S. Beck where my father worked part time. It was always a treat to visit dad at the shoe store. There was a salesgirl named Lilly who always made a big fuss over me. As the rednecks say, "she smelled as purty as the inside of my mamma's purse".

There were many men's clothing shops including Moe Ginsberg and Abe Stark. As a promotion, Abe put up a sign at Ebbets Field, home of the Brooklyn Dodgers. Any batter who hit the sign won a free suit of clothes. Back in the day when baseball players earned less than the Gross National Product of Nicaragua, that was a significant perk. I also recall a men's shop, I think it was called Jack Diamond, next to the Pitkin Theater that was *the* place to shop for the very latest fashions.

A popular Pitkin Avenue destination was Woolworth's or the "five and ten" as we called it. The store had a unique smell, and sold everything from clothes, housewares, toys, beauty products...they even had a snack counter which, as I consider it, is probably where the unique smell came from.

Then there was the Chinese Restaurant, the Wuhan Tea Garden, at Pitkin and Saratoga Avenues, which is the only restaurant I can ever remember going to as a kid. We would get on the Rockaway Avenue trolley, get off at Pitkin Avenue, and meet my father for "Chow Mein". In retrospect, the place was a dump, but at the time, eating out *anywhere* was a treat.

For entertainment we had the Loew's Pitkin Theater. This was a typical old movie house, not as opulent as the Paramount or the Fox theaters in downtown Brooklyn, but compared to the featureless, cinder-block multiplexes of today, it looked like the La Scala opera house...big screen, carpeted staircase, crystal chandeliers, and plush velvet seats.

Pushcart food vendors were common along the avenue selling wonderful treats like candy apples, knishes, shaved ices flavored with sweet syrups and a concoction called a Charlotte Russe, the Brooklyn version of a classic French dessert. It consisted of a round piece of sponge cake topped with gobs of whipped cream and a cherry. It was served in a cardboard container that you ate it out of. To me, it always looked better than it tasted.

Thinking back, these seem like such simple things, but they were the stuff of my childhood. It never ceases to amaze me that the Internet contains so many images and recollections of this time and these places. (You didn't think I actually remembered the name of the Wuhan Tea Garden, did you?)

I'm glad others remembered for me.

Chapter 64:   MEET THE JETSONS

There was a cartoon set in the future called "The Jetsons" that depicted what life would be like in the future. I wonder what my mom could do with the kind of kitchen found in today's modern home? Lots of space filled with granite counters, cooking islands, wondrous appliances and all the technology builders can cram in. Our kitchen in Brooklyn in the 1950's, was a far more modest affair that also doubled as our dining room thanks to a "kitchenette set" of table and chairs. Appliances consisted of the refrigerator, stove and a toaster with folding-down doors...no dishwasher, coffee maker, microwave, blender, or mixer. Our one and only bathroom was located off the kitchen, a room arrangement that, as you can imagine, was not the most convenient.

The kitchen was at the rear of the house and connected to the back yard through a kind of pantry room that was unheated and therefore freezing cold in the winter. The kitchen was small by today's standards, especially since it served as the main focal point for family gatherings, including meals. When company came, they sat at the kitchen table for coffee and cake. As kids we did our homework at the Formica kitchen table since there was really no place else to do it. The table had a leaf stored under it that could stretch the seating capacity to maybe 8 people. In spite of the shortcomings of this "Little House on the Prairie" kitchen, mom managed to crank out three meals a day and knockout holiday dinners.

The fridge was the old type that had to be painstakingly defrosted. Ice would build up in the tiny freezer that held only ice cube trays. If you ever needed a couple of cubes, it meant running the tray under hot water until the thick arctic ice melted sufficiently to pry them out. Frozen foods were not yet a big deal in the Fifties, so there was very little stored in freezers; most people bought fresh food every few days. Our gas stove was a certifiable antique; four burners that had to be lit with a wooden match, and a small oven with no light or timer. Whatever was cooking in the oven had to be watched lest it incinerate. Our toaster had doors that opened so the bread could be exposed to a heating element. There was no timer or pop-up feature so it too had to be watched or you'd be scraping off the charred toast in the sink.

My mother, incredibly, always washed clothes by hand and dried them outside in the back yard. When my younger brother was born in 1953 my father broke down and bought a washing machine. Mom was ecstatic, and carefully read the directions for this, her one and only labor-saving device. Tight quarters meant the washing machine had to be located in the kitchen. (With the bathroom, naturally.) I think mom actually had to run hoses from the sink for her water supply.

We had no dryer, which was fine with me. I used to bury my head in the laundry basket because clean clothes that dried on the clothesline in the sun had the most wonderful smell. It's hard to imagine a simple convenience like a washing machine making a difference in anyone's life, but it did, giving mom more time for the 50 other things she did for us every day.

Maybe one day our grandchildren will reminisce about grandma's old microwave and the tacky refrigerator that didn't even have a frozen Margarita dispenser. There will be no grocery stores or the need to cook; meals will be ordered online and teleported to the dinner table on command. I'm glad I won't be around to see it since I am already regressing technologically. My smart phone mocks me to other smart phones behind my back.

My brother Tony, AKA Zorro, standing next to our Stone Age refrigerator

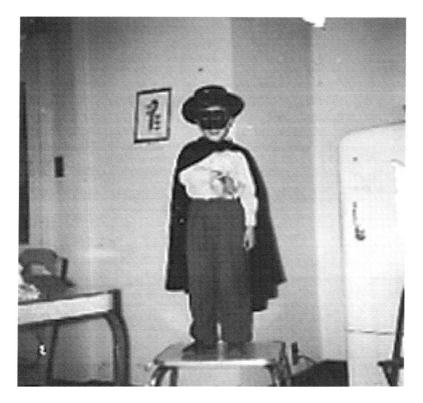

Chapter 65: TRICK OR TREAT

Seeing the little kiddies come to the door dressed in their store-bought Halloween costumes brings a smile to my face. They travel in adult-supervised groups not quite understanding why, despite past admonitions from Mom and Dad, they are being encouraged to take candy from strangers. The younger ones have to be nudged forward by their ever-vigilant parents who accompany the kids on their "Trick or Treat" rounds. Nearby, police squad cars and ambulances full of EMTs are on standby in case one of the tiny Supermans or Ragedy Anns become frightened after timidly ringing the doorbell and having someone they don't know answer.

Things have changed a lot since I was a kid, oh so many years ago. First of all, costumes were for rich kids and sissies. We wore old clothes and blacked our faces with burnt cork for Halloween. There was a practical reason for this since the custom of the time was to fill old socks with flour and mercilessly pound each other until we looked like the ghosts of Christmas past. Also, marking each other with colored chalk, egg throwing and shaving cream pies in the face were popular Halloween activities in the neighborhood.

In those days, trick or treat really meant something. Anybody who was mean enough to begrudge us a piece of candy was very likely to have a stick stuck in their doorbell so it rang continuously. Egging or toilet-papering their house or car was another consequence. A few years ago a group of cute kids came to our door and recited the requisite "Trick or Treat". I jokingly said "trick" and they looked at me with confused faces. Of course I forked over the candy, but not before bemoaning the fact that these unimaginative children were taking all the terror out of Halloween.

My friends and I would have thought we had died and gone to heaven to be able to trick or treat in a neighborhood like ours. Kindly people wait with sack-sized treats and are happy to reward you when you come to their door. The surprising thing is we hardly get any visitors on Halloween. Maybe a few tots who do it more for their parents' gratification than their own; the older kids can't be bothered. The few who do ring the bell are dressed in street clothes and look so bored you want too invite them in to play some video games to restore their spirits.

I can remember like it was yesterday coming home after a night of trick or treating. No parents escorted us; no police cars hovered nearby to protect us; nobody warned us against lunatics who put razor blades into apples and gave them out as treats....we just roamed the streets in our homemade costumes ringing bells and hoping for the best. Candy was never plentiful in our house, not for any nutritional reasons, but anytime my poor mother tried to keep some around, I would search it out and devour it, pretty much like I do today. Opening that shopping bag and gorging ourselves on Mary Janes, Baby Ruths, Three Musketeers Bars, Marshmallow Twists, and even that crappy Candy Corn that makes its appearance around Halloween was the reward for a hard night's work.

As I get older, the mind slips. I can't remember things I meant to do; I ask my wife the same questions over and over; peoples' names and faces escape me. But there must be a place in the mind where treasured memories are stored. A place where things that were so important at some point in your life are kept like carefully wrapped antiques, to be brought out and enjoyed over and over again. Halloween nights in Brooklyn in the 1950s occupy an honored place in that vault.

Chapter 66:   THE NEIGHBORHOOD CRANK

Life changes you. I used to be a lot more fun, but now I'm a cranky old man, just like the ones who used to yell at us when we were kids, and who we taunted in return by ringing their doorbells and running like hell. Sometimes, we might even wedge in a small stick to hold the bell button down so that it rang continuously. We never knew what made these old farts so mean, only that they wouldn't let us come into their yards to retrieve the balls that someone hit in there during a friendly stickball game. There was one real hard case…a nasty, Irish ex-cop…he would take the ball and puncture it with an ice pick before tossing it back with a sneer.

At some point this guy became such an object of hatred that we decided he needed to be taught a lesson. One of the old man's passions was raising pigeons. This was a big hobby in Brooklyn for reasons I could never understand. Pigeons to me are like flying rats, but many people kept pigeon coops on their roofs. A cousin on my father's side had a roomful of trophies he'd won racing pigeons. Personally I found this cousin to be loud and obnoxious, but he became a different man around his birds.

Anyhow our vindictive little brains worked overtime trying to hatch a plot to hit this old crank where it would really hurt…by doing something to his precious pigeons. We thought about poisoning them, but in the end that was ruled out as too drastic. Instead we decided to try to get to the roof where the coops were kept and let the birds out. The job was delegated to an older guy I'll call Joey. Joey was in his late teens, but not quite right in the head; mentally he acted about eight years old. We knew he would do anything we asked of him to win our approval. Kids can be really mean when they put their minds to it.

We waited until our victim left the house to shop. Getting to the roof was no problem. We just sent Joey up onto my roof and waved him down the row of attached houses until he reached the crank's roof half-way down the block. The pigeon coops were closed but not locked. Joey opened one and started waving his arms around to get the birds to fly out. They just stared at him showing no inclination to move. Poor Joey stared down at us not knowing what to do. Meanwhile the lookout we had posted yelled out that the ex-Irish cop had just turned the corner with his groceries and was heading home!

We motioned excitedly to Joey to get out of there, but the poor soul thought we were urging him to work harder, so he just stood there waving energetically as the confused pigeons looked on. It was like the scene in the movie "Rear Window" when Grace Kelly had crossed the courtyard and was in villain Raymond Burr's apartment searching for evidence that he had killed his wife. Just then Burr returns home and is mounting the stairs to the apartment while Jimmy Stewart in the apartment across the way is frantically trying to warn Grace of the danger. We were scared like only kids can be, not knowing what the crank would do to Joey if he ever caught him.

Luckily Joey got tired of trying to free the birds and soon came back down. We were disappointed that our little revenge plot didn't work out, but also very relieved that Joey's guardian angel was on duty that day. We stayed clear of the crank's house for a while after that. Maybe a year later the old man died. I can't say many tears were shed in our crowd. Looking back, I can only wonder (and sympathize a little) what life had done to this man to make him so mean. It kind of sneaks up on you, and before you know it, POW, *you're a crank*.

(Kids should be ringing my bell and running any time now.).

Chapter 67: THE LOST ART OF WALKING

Jerry Seinfeld once commented about the 'people mover conveyors' found at some airports and how folks are content to just allow the mechanism to carry them to their destination. "Do your legs work at all", he wondered. That pretty much sums up how disinclined people are to walk anywhere nowadays. They drive everywhere, no matter how close, to get what they need. Furthermore, they will park in handicapped spaces to avoid walking an extra 50 yards from the regular parking spaces. They will get back in the car and drive to another store in the same strip mall rather than walk the short distance. This unwillingness to walk anywhere is one of the reasons for the alarming obesity trend in this country.

As kids, we walked everywhere. The walk to school every day was maybe 15 minutes; the playground the same. We ran errands for our parents that involved walking to neighborhood stores anywhere from 5 to 20 minutes from home. Longer walks were not uncommon, for example, Highland Park was in Jamaica, maybe a 30 minute walk from home. They had the best baseball fields with real grass and base paths, so we carried our bats and gloves to Jamaica, played a nine-inning game, and then walked home again. The two neighborhood movie theaters were maybe 15 and 20 minute walks from home. There were certainly trains and buses that ran to these destinations, but the nickel fare would also buy any candy bar on the shelf, so we walked.

One of the benefits of walking the neighborhood was that you got to know people. I could start on Rockaway Avenue and walk down Somers Street and tell you who lived in every house all the way down to Stone Avenue. People would greet you as you walked by....How's your mother; don't let me see you again with a cigarette in that mouth; can you go to Louie's and get me a Daily Mirror? These were the exchanges between you and the folks sitting out on their front stoops. Walking also taught you the local streets and how to get around. You knew which block that cute girl lived on, and sometimes walked by just on the chance she'd glance your way. You also knew which blocks it was best to avoid after dark.

In my mind's eye, I can still walk the route to school and church; we must have walked to Callahan and Kelly Park a thousand times to visit the playground, play handball against the wall, or sit on the benches and smoke cigarettes lifted from our fathers' packs. I can see all the mom and pop stores along Pitkin Avenue, our modest shopping Mecca.

My Dad worked there in the A.S. Beck shoe store and I would sometimes pass and wave hello. There was little turnover in those stores; they stayed in the family for generations. We got to know the proprietors, not because we always shopped there but because on our walks we would see them proudly sweeping the street in front of their stores.

I know people who go on vacation and spend all their time at the hotel pool. I am so glad we are still in the habit of walking. When we visit new cities, we are hardly checked into the hotel before we hit the streets for a walk around town. Thankfully our legs do still work and we are happy to have them take us where we want to go.

Chapter 68: JIMMY GETS HIS LICENSE

In the 1950s, just like today, every teen aged guy's biggest dream (well, maybe in *second* place on the teen aged guy dream list) was to get a driver's license. It was embarrassing to pick up your date and head for the subway or the bus stop...not exactly guaranteed to move you up the *cool scale* in your date's eyes. Let's face it, all the really cool guys in the neighborhood drove great cars. Even a dweeb could get girls if he had a hot car. I remember an older guy named "Spike" who was baby-faced, chubby and crew cut, not exactly a James Dean lookalike, but he drove a sleek, yellow and black Mercury with skirt fenders, illuminated wheel wells, and of course the fuzzy dice hanging from the rear-view mirror. What red-blooded girl could resist.

When I turned 17, there was no such thing as "Drivers Ed" in high schools. My father never got his driver's license, so where was I going to learn? I decided to try a driving school, and found one on Pitkin Avenue. It was a small, storefront operation that was run by one guy. When he was out giving lessons, he locked the place up until he got back. I don't remember what he charged, but it couldn't be much. The driving school's "fleet" consisted of one car, a '57 light blue and white Dodge sedan the size of a 747; its tail fins were actually bigger than a 747's.

The lesson was supposed to last an hour, but the owner of the school was going through a nasty divorce from his wife, and the minute we pulled away from the curb, he started ranting about what a tramp she was and how he never should have married her. This was not a short gripe session, but a full-blown, psychotic *rant*. I really didn't need him to teach me how to drive, so I just kept going, with us often winding up in Long Island. We'd get back a couple of hours later, the driving instructor felt better after venting about his no-good wife, and I got in a couple of solid hours practice on the big Dodge.

When I was ready to take my driver's test, the instructor met me at the test site, which I think was at the deserted end of Pennsylvania Avenue where Starrett City is now located. The applicants lined up at the curb waiting for the test administrator to call their names and go out for their road test. There was a space at the curb of maybe 50 yards between the cars returning from their tests, and behind them, the cars still waiting to pull out for theirs. I was second in line to be called. The test administrator got into the car immediately in front of mine. The driver of the car floored the accelerator, covered that 50 yard gap in a flash, and *rear-ended* the car in front of him. The test administrator calmly got out, wrote something on the lunatic's test application form, and coolly waved me up. I guess those guys had seen it all.

I did better than the guy before me. I signaled for turns, kept both hands on the wheel at "10 and 2" executed a perfect U-turn and finished with a flawless parallel park. They weren't supposed to tell you if you passed or not, but the test administrator, relieved I guess that I didn't crash the car, said: "You did OK kid". I was beside myself with joy. The two weeks or so it took for that license to come in the mail seemed like forever. When it arrived, I was overjoyed; no more subway dates. Well except for one small detail...I now had a license, *but no car.* This was a mere technicality, as I soon talked my unsuspecting father into going halves with me on a new '61 Chevy Impala.

Kids today start taking Driver's Ed at age 16 or earlier, and Daddy usually provides them with a car by the time they graduate high school. It's almost an entitlement in their minds. They could never understand what having a car meant to us back then. We washed it every Saturday, waxed it under the el where it was shady, and tricked it out with any accessories we could afford. The car became an extension of our personality, not just transportation, but a magic carpet that carried us to exotic places filled with wondrous things we never saw much in the neighborhood, like *trees*. If you don't believe me, go to a classic car show and ask any owner to tell you about his "baby". Be prepared to stay a while.

Me around the age I took my driver's test

Chapter 69: THE PREPPIES AND THE HOODS

If you saw the movie "West Side Story" you may remember that one of the plot lines was the friction between two street gangs, The Sharks and The Jets. There were gangs around for sure in the Fifties in our neighborhood, but they couldn't dance like the gangs in this movie! In my neighborhood we saw an interesting phenomenon around the time Pat Boone started to become popular. Up until then, guys tended to dress in regular street clothes, or if they identified with James Dean in "Rebel Without a Cause" like I did, they wore black leather jackets, dungarees (not jeans) and motorcycle boots. Although I sported the "hood" look, I was a fraud. I was just a regular guy trying to fit in.

When Pat Boone arrived on the scene, I noticed a change in the way guys were dressing. Pat was the personification of the clean-cut kid, the anti-Elvis, and parents and kids alike embraced him. Maybe Pat could help stem the tide of Rock and Roll, the devil's music. Maybe if our kids had someone popular they could emulate, we still had a chance to save their souls. In my high school, black jackets and boots began to disappear as button-down shirts and white bucks or saddle shoes took their place. Long hair with duck-tails got cut and hair was styled more like Pat's, parted neatly and combed to the side. Dungarees were out and chino pants with that little belt across the back were in. The Preppies were taking on The Hoods and winning.

I resisted, mainly because I thought Pat Boone was not even in the same league as James Dean. He was polite instead of sullen; neatly groomed instead of a slob; and sang songs about lollypops and moonbeams...I hated him. But soon my friends began to switch sides. I hardly recognized them in their sissy shoes and school sweaters. I held out as long as I could, but as the hood clique faded away like Neanderthal man, I became more and more conspicuous. Nobody wanted to hang out with a hood anymore, even a fake one. Teachers looked on hoods as trouble back in the day when they still had some actual authority to make your life difficult. But the straw that broke the camel's back was when most of the good looking girls moved into the Preppie table in the cafeteria. I had no choice but to cave.

When I asked my mother if I could but some new clothes, she resisted because money was tight. When I told her I wanted to try button-down shirts and chinos however, she muttered her thanks to Our Lady of Mount Carmel and we went to Mays Department Store. Now I show up in school in Preppie garb and it feels It like my worlds were colliding. I am a teenage sellout.

The Preppie crowd was suspicious of my sudden conversion, and my hood friends looked at me like the Benedict Arnold I was. I didn't belong anywhere. Although I still harbored hood sympathies, by sheer strength of will, I out-prepped the Preppies. My acceptance came when I was allowed to sit at her cafeteria table with Sheila, Jewish American Princess and Queen of the Preppies. Ironically, having finally earned my white bucks, it slowly dawned on me that this was really not my crowd. Luckily, graduation day arrived and I went out into the world still not quite sure of who I was.

I guess the person who finally helped me find myself was my wife. After dating on and off for a few years, I realized that what I wanted in life was to spend the rest of it with her. I proposed and gave her an engagement ring while on a carriage ride in Central Park. This move was right out of the manual: "Romantic Gestures for the Clueless". Happily for me she accepted and has helped shape who I am ever since. Any good qualities or instincts I may have probably came from her. My bad points I attribute to the Hood-Preppie conflict that raged in me during those formative teen years.

She has been at it for nearly 48 years now and still has work to do. I am very lucky that she never gave up on me.

Chapter 70: LIFE'S MILESTONES

All humans enter this world at birth and leave it at death, hopefully going on to a better place where they have plasma TVs in every room and never heard of "The View". For me life was marked by certain events and rituals, the hallmarks of growing up in an Italian-American family. These were happy times, and as I think back on them I can recall the joy that each event inspired. Most of us pass through these gateways on our march through life, but for Italian-Americans, the flavor is a little different something like putting fennel seed in your meatballs to make them a cut above the ordinary.

I was born the first child of Frances and Anthony Pantaleno in Unity Hospital in Brooklyn, New York on July 5, 1942. My parents named me James. They didn't give me a middle name because we couldn't afford one. I can just imagine the scene on Pacific Street when they brought me home. The anisette cookies and the bottle of Fleishman's Rye would have been out as family and friends filed in to see the baby and congratulate the parents. There probably was also an old woman in black performing some Italian black-magic ritual to ensure health and wealth for the baby. The spell was half effective.

In the second grade I received my first Holy Communion. This was a big event in Catholic-Italian households, although not as big as today when spending on communion parties exceeds what I spent on my wedding. We were drilled by our teachers at Our Lady of Lourdes in preparation for the event. Then, on the big day, we marched down the aisle in that magnificent church, boys on one side, girls on the other. The host was placed on our tongues while kneeling at the altar rail (no receiving communion in the hand back then) and we marched back to our assigned pews as our proud families looked on. It was customary to capture such special events for posterity in a formal studio portrait, which is shown at left.

The next big milestone was Confirmation, which I received in the sixth grade. This is the next step in a Catholic boy's development. The event required that all boys buy a dark blue suit. My mother took me to Klein's on Union Square in Manhattan, where we bought a suit sized so big (so I wouldn't outgrow it too quickly) that I think I wore it to my first job interview. We were allowed to choose a "Confirmation Name" and I chose Philip in tribute to my good friend and next-door neighbor. My grandmother pulled me aside when we got home from church and slipped me a dollar. (Note the column I'm standing next to is the same as for my Communion picture. Thank you, Roma Studios.)

I graduated grammar school and was headed to Brooklyn Technical High School, (see Chapter 59.) I was torn between Tech and Bishop Loughlin High School, whose entrance exam I had passed. After 8 years I was tired of the discipline of Catholic school and decided on Tech. Big Mistake. I needed the discipline I would not get at Tech to do well. I drifted into bad company at Tech and had to leave six months before graduation to finish up elsewhere. I sometimes wonder if life would have turned out differently if I had gone to Loughlin.

At age 24, I married Jasmine, the love of my life. We had dated for a while after being introduced by friends, but then separated for a few years. At the wedding of those friends, Jasmine was the maid of honor and I was the best man. I didn't let her get away a second time. I had brought girls home before, but this time my mother pulled me aside and said: "This is the one". How can a boy argue with his mother. We were wed at St. Francis Xavier church in Brooklyn followed by a rousing reception at The Pisa, on 86th Street. Pictured with us is the couple who introduced us all those years ago on a trip to Italy. I owe them a lot.

Less than ten months after the wedding, (hey, we're Italian) our daughter Laura was born. She was the most beautiful little girl I ever saw. Four years later came our son Michael, who arrived after a thrill-packed, police-escorted ride to the hospital. After another four year interval, our youngest son Matthew was born to complete our family. (We always kidded that the four years between each child was our college tuition payment plan). In time, son-in-law Malcolm, daughter-in-law Alicia, and daughter-in-law to be (this September) Tara joined the family. Our granddaughter Ava arrived in 2003, and immediately took over all family operations, and our second granddaughter, Priscilla, was born this past January. We have been blessed. As the Italians say, "Alla famiglia".

P.S. I won't be around to write about the final milestone in my life. Somebody say something nice.

Me in my oversized Confirmation suit

Looking earnest in my cap and gown. Needed an eyebrow waxing.

Chapter 71:   FUN WITH DICK AND JANE

Caution: This post is for real old timers only. In an age when printed books as we know them are disappearing in favor of digital editions, I was remembering my parochial school days in the '40s and '50s when none of this electronic stuff had even been imagined. Books were valued and treated with loving care. Most households struggled to put food on the table, so for many, books were a luxury.

We had a few well-thumbed volumes in our house, but most of the books I read came from the public library. My parents were too busy raising us and making ends meet to have much free time for reading. The first books I came in contact with were the "Dick and Jane" readers we were given in first grade. The idyllic lives led by Dick and Jane, their parents, their dog Spot and cat Tabby were so far removed from my own Italian-American upbringing. They needed a version for my neighborhood called "Fun with Vito and Theresa"..

We received a new reader in every grade. The stories got more sophisticated as we were introduced to harder vocabulary words and more complex sentence structure. We stood up and read aloud in the classroom, with our teachers calling on each child to take a turn. If you mispronounced a word, the teacher would correct you, and so we learned. (Today's parents would probably be consulting attorneys to sue the school for publicly correcting their child in class.) The readers were given to you at the beginning of each term, and you were responsible for caring for them. I remember making book covers out of brown paper bags to help protect the book covers. You had to turn the books in at the end of the term, and God help you if there was any scribbled marks on the pages.

We also wrote with fountain pens, the kind you had to fill with ink. The pens had a rubber bladder that held about a day's worth of brilliant thoughts. We used blotters to blot the ink while it was still wet to keep it from smearing. All the local politicians handed out blotters with their campaign pictures on the reverse side of the blotting paper. We were required to use only blue-black ink in our pens. You were expected to fill your pen at home, but the teachers kept a supply of ink you could use if you ran out. Scripto made blue-black ink, but then a company called Waterman's began making inks in exotic colors like aqua and green, colors which were frowned upon in our school. Because the pens tended to leak, every boy at one time or other wore his blue-black badge of courage with honor.

I have a tablet, laptop, smart phone and a Dick Tracy two-way wrist radio, but like some old timers, I still like the feel and smell of real books.

Chapter 72:   L.S.M.F.T.

If you were around in the fifties, you may remember that L.S.M.F.T. stands for "Lucky Strike Means Fine Tobacco". Lucky Strike (or Luckies) were one of the many cigarette brands that thrived after WWII. Even during the war they sent Luckies in the new white package to troops overseas with the slogan: "Lucky Strike Green goes to war". The original Luckies pack was green in color, but during the war, chromium (an essential ingredient in green ink) was in short supply, so Luckies switched to a white pack and never changed back. No, no, don't thank me. I am here to enlighten.

Cigarettes were still glamorous in the fifties. Every movie star, from tough-talking gangsters to beautiful leading ladies happily puffed away on screen. It's no wonder that most kids couldn't wait to light up their first cigarette. Smoking was a rite of passage for us. I started smoking around age 11 or 12. I would snitch one from my father's pack or (germophobes please stop reading here) pick up a butt in the street that still had a few puffs left in it. What, you didn't have any disgusting habits?

Cigarettes were boldly advertised in the fifties...even doctors promoted them. There were ashtrays in every room of every house. Unlike today when smokers have to sneak into an alley for their fix, smoking was permitted everywhere: airplanes, office buildings, theaters, even hospital rooms; you were free to have a smoke pretty much anywhere. Of course a pack of cigarettes cost about a quarter back then, so two packs a day was no big financial burden. The last time I checked, to buy a carton of cigarettes you needed a co-signer for the loan.

Ad agencies were at their creative best when selling cigarettes including the memorable Dancing Old Gold pack. Dennis James was the spokesman for this brand. Well known personalities like future President Ronald Reagan, Frank Sinatra, Arthur Godfrey, Lucille Ball, John Wayne, Joan Fontaine, and Humphrey Bogart hawked cigarettes. Baseless scientific claims were another favorite tactic. Make-believe doctors extolled the "Scientific Evidence" on the beneficial effects of smoking Chesterfields.

One of the most successful and long-running ad campaigns was for Marlboro. The "Marlboro Man" became the new yardstick for manly good looks. Guys who smoked Marlboros could identify with the rugged cowboys of the old West. I dumped my old brand in a heartbeat to proudly join the swelling ranks of the Marlboro Men.

I know it's not a popular notion today, but I enjoyed smoking. There was nothing like a cigarette with my morning coffee or after a satisfying meal. If they could figure out a way to make cigarettes harmless, I'd run out and buy a carton of Marlboros in a minute. That is if I could get a co-signer for the loan.

Chapter 73:   UNCLE SAM WANTS ME?

When I graduated high school at the age of 17, I had no plans to enter college and no clue what to do with my life. The war in Viet Nam was just heating up, and the military draft was still very much in place for healthy young men. Having a serious aversion to bullets, I decided on a preemptive strike and joined the U.S. Army Reserves. At the time it seemed like the safest alternative to being drafted. So, in May 1960, two months shy of my eighteenth birthday, my father "Tony Boots" walked me to the subway station. My dad had never given me the "birds and bees" talk. As I shook hands with him before descending the steps, he pressed two condoms into my palm and asked: "Do you know what these are for?" I dumbly nodded yes, and he walked away slowly, mentally crossing off another item on his parenting "to do" list.

When they tested me at the recruitment center, as they do all new recruits, they determined that my M.O.S. (Military Occupational Specialty) was Medic. My friend Lefty was assigned an M.O.S. of Cook. Having grown up in an Italian household on Hull Street eating his mother Dolly's cooking was his main qualification for this assignment. Lefty and I left for Fort Dix, New Jersey, and although we would later be assigned to North Carolina and Texas respectively to pursue advanced training in our different M.O.S.'s (Military Occupational Specialty), I was glad he would be with me for eight weeks of basic training. Contrary to all the guys who bitch about Army basic training, I loved it. I was seventeen years old and just too dumb to know any better. I was in great shape with a 33 inch waist and an athlete's body. They gave us free clothes, guns to play with, and all the food you could eat, so I just did what I was told and went with the program.

The older guys in my company complained constantly about how dumb the Army was and adopted an air of superiority over the regular Army staff who were training us. Even at seventeen, I sensed the folly of this attitude; it only made the redneck Sergeants want to torment us more. One Corporal in particular made it clear that as a Louisiana boy, he had no use for smart-aleck Northerners, especially Eye-tal-ians as he sneeringly pronounced it. This guy was tall and skinny and as mean as they get. He went out of his way to make our lives a living hell, and in the Army, someone with one stripe more than you is your *lord and master.* I did my best to stay out of his way, but I came in for my share of crap. Only a bit of serendipity saved me from eight whole weeks of pain.

I think it was Irving Berlin who wrote a song called: "Send a Salami to Your Boy in the Army", and that's exactly what my mother used to do. Every week she sent me a box of goodies from home, and always included a pepperoni. One Saturday afternoon we were off duty and, since I had no weekend pass to leave the base, I was moping around the barracks. I had the pepperoni out and was snacking when this Corporal walked over: "Whatcha eatin' Panalena" (Southern for Pantaleno). I told him and offered him some. He was amazed that something Eye-tal-ian could taste so good. Said it reminded him of the Andouille sausages they ate back home.

We finished the pepperoni together and a strange bond was formed. In conversation he turned out to be a decent guy who was as homesick as the rest of us. I was golden from that day forward. Every once in a while he would ask" "Hey Panalena, got any of that pepperona", and of course, like some drug pusher in a back alley, I had.

(New recruits: Lefty, Me, Ronnie)

Chapter 74:   ARMY DAYS, CONTINUED

Basic training passed pretty quickly. In the Army there is always something going on, even if it's only polishing shoes and brass buckles. We spent hours cleaning the barracks and surrounding grounds. The purpose of this 8 week period is to get soldiers used to one thing only, obeying orders, no matter how illogical they may seem. I guess if we were ever in the heat of battle, there was no room for debate; if the Lieutenant said "Take that hill" you jumped out of your foxhole and ran toward the hill. Thank God I was never called upon to go into combat. It must be a horrific experience. Toward the end of our training, we were all tired and needed a break.

Come July 4th weekend, our unit was detailed to march that Saturday in a parade down in Wildwood, New Jersey. This wasn't quite as good as getting a weekend pass, but it was better than hanging around the base. The day started out rainy, so we wore our Army raincoats over our uniforms. Luckily the sun came out before we set off, and we were able to leave our raincoats on the bus before marching in the ninety degree heat. The order of march for the parade was set, with military units from surrounding bases sending contingents of sailors, airmen, and marines to march with us soldiers. Our unit was just ahead of the Army Marching Band, and everyone was grousing; not only were we marching in full dress uniforms in this miserable heat, but we had to be subjected to hours of John Philip Sousa marches!

As we set off the people pressed forward to watch us go by. The Army Band struck up: "When the Caissons Go Rolling Along". Suddenly there were faces smiling out on us, little kids were running down the sidewalks waving their tiny American flags, and veterans of past wars were holding their hats or their hands over their hearts. It was a scene right out of a Norman Rockwell painting. In an instant, the soldiers all around me stood up straighter and stepped out a little livelier. The grousing stopped because we all had lumps in out throats. Forgotten were the 20-mile night marches with full backpacks, the hours spent shining shoes and polishing brass buckles, even the mean-spirited Sergeants who forced screw-ups to clean latrines with their tooth brushes...we were soldiers in the United States Army, at that moment feeling honored and privileged to be serving our country.

After the parade, our officers gave us permission to stay in town for the rest of the day as long as we returned in time to catch the bus back to the base. Wildwood is a small, sleepy town in the winter, but back then in the summer time, it becomes *party central*. Being young men with a great fondness for alcohol, we did our best to deplete the town's supply. We made the bus just in time to collapse asleep in the hard seats.

Upon arrival at Fort Dix, we grabbed our raincoats and left the bus. It had started to drizzle so I put the raincoat on to protect my uniform. I soon noticed soldiers throwing snappy salutes my way. I saluted back being too groggy to wonder why they were saluting a lowly buck private. It was then that I glanced down and saw the shiny silver bars on my lapels; I had taken my Lieutenant's raincoat by mistake, and it was his insignia of rank drawing all the salutes. I enjoyed my fifteen minutes of fame, but hurriedly rushed to the orderly room to explain the error before I wound up in the brig for impersonating an officer.

Military service was good for me. It helped me to learn how to get along on my own, and how to be part of a team where each person did his share for the success of all. I think a year of national service of some sort should be mandatory for young people, even before entering college. There is a lot of good work to be done, and it is a small price to pay for living in the greatest country in the world.

Pvt. James Pantaleno, 356th Station Hospital, U.S. Army Medical Corps

Chapter 75:   ARMY DAYS, TEXAS STYLE

After 8 weeks of Basic Training at Fort Dix, I learned I was headed for Fort Sam Houston in San Antonio, Texas. This is where U.S. Army Medical Corpsman received their advanced training back in 1960. I was excited. I had barely been out of Brooklyn up until then, much less to an exotic place like Texas. After a short leave at home, I said goodbye to the family and lugged my giant duffel bag to Kennedy Airport. It was still called Idlewild Airport back them before they renamed it in honor of JFK in 1963.

My flight was on Braniff Airlines, a fairly new carrier that was becoming famous for its wildly colored airplanes and pretty stewardesses. I was in uniform for the flight and was mildly surprised when the crew treated me with such deference. Those were the days of free booze and my glass was never empty. It was also the days of real food on airplanes and I thought the meal was fantastic. I had nothing to compare this flight to, and thought it was magical.

Upon landing and being transported to Fort Sam in San Antonio, I was pleasantly surprised to see how differently soldiers were treated at the base compared to the rotten treatment we got at Fort Dix. It was more professional and businesslike and the change was nice to see. The barracks we lived in were Spartan, but a cut above our quarters in Basic Training. After settling in, I quickly made friends with three guys who would be my posse for the remainder of our stay in Texas.

Ed was from Philadelphia and I had no idea what he did in civilian life. He was Italian, handsome and gregarious, an easy guy to befriend. He spoke with that unique Philly accent that clanked on a New Yorker's ear. Then there were Sydney and Melvin, both Jewish pharmacists, Syd from Atlanta, Georgia, and Mel from Syracuse, New York. The four of us made an interesting dynamic; two Italians and two Jews trying to survive in a place where anyone who didn't speak with a drawl was immediately suspect. All were older than my 18 years and acted like older brothers to keep an eye on me.

Our daily routine was mindlessly unchanged. Up early for breakfast (contrary to popular belief, Army food was very good) and then off to class. Most of the classes for medical corpsmen dealt with giving first aid on the battlefield, We learned "triage", the art of sorting and prioritizing injured soldiers. We learned to splint bones, treat burns, bind wounds and evacuate casualties from the field. One day during a class on evacuating the wounded by helicopter, the instructor asked for a volunteer to play the role of injured soldier. I jumped up, violating the soldier's unspoken oath of "never volunteer". I thought it would be a nice free helicopter ride. I didn't realize it would be on a stretcher strapped to the landing struts outside the chopper. We took off and after a brief, terrifying ride, landed. I changed my underwear and class continued.

Once Ed and I were assigned to KP or Kitchen Police. This is an army term for kitchen duty. It is miserable. We worked like dogs all day in a hot kitchen scrubbing pots and pans, and by 7 pm were exhausted. After some deliberation we decided to head into San Antonio for a beer. As tired as we were it sounded like a good idea. We had no passes to get off the base but decided a quick beer couldn't get us into trouble. Problem was the base MPs, Military Police, were making rounds of local bars that night checking passes and we were caught. After a disciplinary hearing by our commanding officer we received an Article 15, the Army equivalent of a misdemeanor. for being AWOL (Absent Without Leave). There went my dream of making General.

Army life wasn't all bad. Sydney had driven from Georgia to Texas in a white Oldsmobile convertible the size of a 747. When we left the base, we drove out in style, top down and hair blowing in the hot Texas sun. We sometimes took trips into nearby Mexico just to break the monotony of base life. I remember driving to Monterrey and not being all that impressed. We sometimes stayed at I think it was a Best Western motel. I remember lying out by the pool with a cold Lone Star beer in my hand soaking up rays and listening to Frank Sinatra sing Moonlight in Vermont over the loudspeakers. Army life was sweeter than I imagined it could ever be.

I often wonder what Ed, Syd and Mel are doing these days? They were good buddies who helped make Army life actually enjoyable for me. When I got home after being released from active duty, I was obligated to do seven and a half more years of reserve duty. We met once a month at an armory down on Christopher Street in Greenwich Village and also attended two-week summer camps at Camp Drum upstate New York. It was inconvenient, but thankfully my reserve unit was never called up.

I guess the most valuable thing I took away from Army life was how to add salted peanuts to a cold Dr. Pepper soda for a delicious snack.

Chapter 76: STEVE THE JUNKMAN

A few doors down from my house in Brooklyn lived Steve the Junkman. That's what everyone called him; his profession became part of his identity. In a time when people still actually fixed things instead of throwing them away, Steve collected junk and gave it new life. He was good with his hands and sold his second-hand creations at bargain prices. He would have a field day if he lived today. I see the perfectly good things that people throw away and think of Steve.

In the summer, Steve put the junk business on hold and moved into the more exotic fruit business. His horse-drawn wagon (after a good cleaning I hope) became a travelling fruit store, and he meandered around the neighborhood announcing his presence by ringing a cowbell. Steve bought his fruit from the local stores probably a day before it became inedible, and tried peddling it before it imploded. His skin was wrinkled and mahogany colored from hours of sitting in the sun making his rounds, I'm almost certain Steve had a wife, but in all the years we lived near him, I can't recall ever seeing her. Maybe he kept her in the cellar like Mrs. Bates.

Steve was a wild-looking guy with a shock of white hair and very crabby, so mostly us kids steered clear of him. He or his horse (depending on how good your aim was) were often targets of a winter snowball... maybe that's why he was nasty to us. Anyhow, as he motioned me toward him one day, you can understand my reluctance to obey. He gave me a smile (I could tell because his tooth was showing) and I slowly approached as my boyish caution turned to curiosity. He reached down and picked up a handful of oats that had spilled from his horse's feedbag. Handing them to me, he instructed me to plant them in my back yard, water them, and watch what happened.

Normally, I probably would have just taken and thrown them away when Steve wasn't looking. This day must have been an awfully slow day for be because I actually planted the oats in our back yard. Maybe I could grow a horse! Imagine my delight when a couple of weeks passed and the planted oats produced beautiful green grass. No agricultural college graduate ever felt closer to the land than I did that day. The next day I thanked Steve for my lesson in Farming 101. He gave me a wink and a toothless grin.

Steve had a married daughter living with him whose husband was away serving in Korea. On another slow day in the neighborhood, we were going through people's garbage pails. (Talk about a new low...going through a junk man's trash.) One of my friends came across a packet of love letters written to Steve's daughter by her soldier-boy husband. He must have been extremely horny over there because these letters contained the most intimate and lurid details about their love life. I realize today what a terrible thing we did, but back then, to a bunch of pre-teen boys, this was like finding gold.

Steve's daughter was a rather plain-looking girl who would not get a second look walking down the street. After those letters made the rounds though, she never lacked for an all-too-willing kid to carry her groceries home. Wherever you are Steve's daughter, I apologize for this unbelievable intrusion into your personal life.

Chapter 77:   DINNER CHOICES: TAKE IT OR LEAVE IT

The food police are driving me crazy. Every day there's a new rule I'm supposed to follow. No red meat, don't eat white flour, can't eat fruit with a meal, don't eat after 8 pm, avoid fast food, wine is bad, wine is good...enough already. There are more special diets than you can shake a pork chop at: Atkins, Miami Beach, Weight Watchers, Jenny Craig, Slim-Fast, and all will ultimately fail. Our bodies need all kinds of foods for nutrition, and to fool your body into losing weight by eating grapefruit three times a day is ridiculous. Then there are the supplements being peddled. The great and powerful Dr. Oz tells people to drink dandelion juice while walking backwards clockwise in circles and the idiots can't order it fast enough...sometimes from Dr. Oz's own website...no conflict of interest there.

When I was growing up, we ate well in spite of not having acre-sized supermarkets and owning refrigerators the size of Buicks. There were no microwave ovens, no lean cuisines, no fast food joints and no Costco warehouses where you could buy 80 frozen burgers at a clip. Our mothers shopped at local stores for meat, fish, bread, eggs, fruit and vegetables. We didn't have a pantry full of snack chips in bags the size of pillows. There were no gallon-sized ice cream containers in our freezers because they would never fit with the six inches of ice built up around the ice cube trays...the only things in the freezer!

We bought what we needed for a few days and used it all; nothing went to waste. Bones, bits and scraps went into soups, omelets, even pies. (If you never tasted escarole pie or spaghetti pie, your life is sadly incomplete.) I get a kick out of parents who fret when little Madison refuses to eat his or her dinner and demands something else. Our alternatives were peanut butter or go hungry. We ate what was put in front of us, period. There were times when, maybe on days close to Dad's next paycheck, we couldn't afford to buy meat. Not a problem; Mom had a dozen meatless dishes that could give a good steak a run for its money. Pasta with lentils, peas, potatoes, broccoli, eggplant or chick peas. Eggs with peppers, potatoes, spinach, or cheese. They were cheap to prepare, but delicious, nutritious and satisfying.

I hear people ordering meals in restaurants that come with a page and a half of verbal instructions. Can you please ask the chef to make that with no gluten, no wheat, no salt, no peanuts, no dairy and no MSG. Also, can that be baked instead of fried, and instead of the French fries can I have cabbage roots. Can you tell me if these dishes were washed in organic soap? On a recent trip to Italy we had a woman on our tour who carried her own little food packets with her and drove the waiters crazy because she was a vegan. I remember thinking, here we are in one of the world's best places to get great food and this ditz is sprinkling pistachio nuts on her pasta instead of the great sauce that normally accompanied it.

I'm not chastising people who have legitimate, medically confirmed food allergies and have to watch what they eat, I'm talking about the crowd who has to follow Dr. Oz's latest food commandment just to be trendy. They move from diet to diet and fad to fad hoping to get healthier or lose weight, but they are badly misguided. What it all comes down to is "pie-hole control" ... calories in minus calories burned off exercising equals what's left of you. Back in the Fifties, we walked everywhere. Restaurant portions did not feed four. You could not pick up the phone and have bags of food dropped off at your door. Dinner choices were two…take it or leave it. You ate real food, fresh-cooked and in moderation. Write that down...it's the secret to good health and a trimmer waistline.

I always got a big kick out of the scene in Woody Allen's movie, "Sleeper" where doctors from the future were discussing how wrong we were in the past to avoid certain foods like hot fudge sundaes which, as they now knew, were actually good for you.

Chapter 78:   THE ART OF IMAGINING

I try putting these little essays about growing up in the 1950's out there in the hope that one day some bored kid will read them and marvel at what it was like to grow up in a time when sometimes, all we had to play with came straight from our imaginations. There were no acre-sized Toys 'R Us stores where every conceivable toy was on the shelves, complete with instructions, and safety warnings not to ingest small plastic parts. Fifties kids may have been short on cash, but they had this amazing ability to make games out of nothing. City neighborhoods offered no trees to climb, no streams to fish in and no caves to explore. It took the ingenuity of generations of street kids to invent games that could be played anywhere for free.

I have returned to this idea often because it occurs to me that we are depriving modern children from ever having to stretch their brains to create ways to amuse themselves that don't involve televisions, computers, video games and smart phones. It would be interesting to me to fill a room with today's ten-year-olds and give them things like a length of rope, a rubber ball, a stick or an empty cardboard box just to see what games they can improvise. Their lives are so structured and supervised, I wonder if they could do it. Do they ever have time, between organized activities, play dates and incessant homework, to just lay down in the grass and try to see shapes in the fleecy white clouds hanging up in the sky?

I won't repeat what I've said before about how many games we played using only a rubber ball...known colloquially in the hood as a Spal-deen. Suffice to say there were at least 25 games to amuse us. We spent hours playing games like Hide and Seek, Johnny on the Pony, Red Light-Green Light, Kick the Can, Giant Steps, and Ring-a-levio. Total cost to play: zero. On rainy days we would have Popsicle stick races in the fast-flowing streams of water that raced along the curb in the street. If somebody on the block got a new refrigerator or washing machine, the empty box put out in the trash became a castle or a rocket ship. On snowy days we would "borrow" the sturdy metal garbage can covers from unsuspecting neighbors and use them as sleds.

We would roll an old tire down the hill, sometimes riding in it and staggering around dizzy afterward. Any fence, no matter how high, even those topped with barbed wire, became our Matterhorn. On really slow days we would sneak on the elevated trains that ran out to Jamaica in Queens. Some enterprising soul had pried open the heavy black bars that protected the unattended Fulton Street station just wide enough for skinny kids to fit through.

First the crew-cut head, then the torso, and finally the legs passed through the opening. One day, a chubbier kid got his head through, but couldn't fit the rest of himself. The cops were called to get him out, and we all received a stern lecture, but the spectacle entertained the rest of us for a couple of hours. Total cost: free.

The stoop (a flight of steps outside a house) was our permanent hangout. We played cards, sneaked cigarettes, girl-watched, and yelled derogatory remarks at passers-by...all free. As lame as it may sound today, we played a game called "movie star initials" that involved taking turns giving the initials of an unnamed screen star, and having to guess the identity of the actor/actress. We would make small bets on the make or color of the next car to turn the corner. Sometimes in desperation we would join the girls' jump-rope games. They were usually happy to have us thinking we were finally showing some interest in them until we started horsing around and were sent packing with slaps and giggles.

As I read this I shake my head realizing how awful these silly games must sound to today's kids who seem to enjoy themselves only when there is a joystick in hand. My childhood was a delight because everything we needed for a good time we carried around in our heads. Here's to the vanishing power of imagination.

Chapter 79:   SUMMERTIME AND THE LIVING IS SWEATY

Summer in the city has always been rough, but in the 1950s, air-conditioning existed pretty much in movie theaters only; everywhere else you had to rely on your imagination to keep cool. This was back in the day before casual business dress, so any poor schlub in an office job had to put on a suit and tie and descend into Dante's Seventh Circle of Hell, otherwise known as the NYC subway system. As sweaty commuters stood cheek-to-cheek reading the Miss Rheingold ads, ancient fans would blow very hot air into their faces at 60 miles an hour. Women divided their time between fighting off gropers and keeping their foot-high beehive hairdos from collapsing in the hot Santa Ana winds.

I guess toward the end of the 1950's, office buildings began to install air conditioning, so at least oppressed employees climbing up out of steamy subway stations could get that blast of resuscitating cold air as they hit their building lobbies. People who weren't lucky enough to work in offices got little relief during the long, hot summers. It was especially rough for people like firefighters who had to don 50 pounds of heavy gear to fight fires, or cops who wore those old-fashioned wool police uniforms that buttoned up to the neck. Construction workers and utility workers also suffered (as they still do today) by not only laboring in the heat, but often in holes in the ground that intensified their discomfort.

Kids too had to find ways to beat the heat. Going to the beach was great if your parents were in the mood to take you. I remember well the ride to Coney Island, first on the A train from our local Rockaway Avenue station to Franklin Avenue where we changed for the elevated Brighton line. The backs of your legs stuck to the straw train seats as you took what felt like an interminable ride to our destination, Coney Island Avenue. Then a walk up narrow streets past the tacky souvenir shops, then under the shade of the boardwalk onto the hot sand where you did the "beach blanket mambo" (stepping on the corners of other people's blankets to avoid scorching your feet) until finally, looming on the hazy horizon, the cool Atlantic ocean appeared.

Kids found other ways to cool off like going to the local playground to romp in the wading pool. This was a bowl-shaped concrete enclosure with shower sprays of water shooting out of openings around the "pool", which held maybe two inches of water. If you fell while frolicking in this cement death trap, a trip to the emergency room was a real possibility. We also opened street hydrants, or Johnnie pumps as we called them, and created our own little asphalt beach. Kids came pouring out of hot brick houses to play in the street. Sneakers were a good idea to help prevent stepping on rocks or broken glass. (See trip to emergency room.) Unsuspecting cars rolling slowly down the block with open windows were considered fair game. Evil boys used tin cans to direct the stream of the water gushing from the hydrant into 1954 Chevys, and then ran like hell.

If putting a man on the moon was ranked as man's greatest challenge, then teaching summer school physics in non-air-conditioned classrooms to disinterested kids who had already failed it once must have come in a close second. I remember enduring this fate in high school. I can still see the anguished face of the poor teacher who had sacrificed, gone to college, and became an educator in the hope of improving young minds. He was reduced nearly to tears by a room full of young thugs who wanted no part of Einstein's Theory of Relativity and who thought Sir Isaac Newton was the guy they named the cookie after. To make matters worse, the class was given at New Utrecht High School, located a few short train stops from Coney Island. We could almost smell the hot dogs from Nathan's wafting in on the breeze coming through the open window.

Anyone reading this might get the mistaken impression that summers in the 1950's in Brooklyn were terrible. In fact, they were glorious, and I wouldn't trade those memories for anything. (OK, maybe for a red, Jaguar XKE but nothing else.)

Chapter 80: DROPPING THE DIME

When I tried to locate the origin of the phrase "dropping the dime", I found out that surprisingly, it has many meanings. The definition that most closely corresponds to my understanding of the term was found in the Slang Dictionary: To inform on or betray someone as in "Rocky dropped the dime on Knuckles to save his own skin". This expression, alluding to the ten cent coin long used in pay phones for making a telephone call, originated as underworld slang for phoning the police to inform on a criminal, and occasionally is used to describe *any* kind of betrayal.

In the Brooklyn street culture of the 1950s, snitching on anyone about anything was frowned upon. The code was followed by any kid who wanted to belong...you just didn't drop the dime on a comrade if you wanted to retain their trust. Any kid who betrayed the code and ratted someone out was likely to be shunned by the group and maybe even retaliated against with the administration of a schoolyard beating to remind him of the rules. One possible origin for the rule of silence might be the Sicilian code of "Omertà" as described below by Mafia researcher Antonio Cutrera.

"The basic principle of Omertà is that it is not "manly" to seek the aid of legal authorities to settle personal grievances. The suspicion of being a "stool pigeon" (an informant), constituted the blackest mark against manhood. Each wronged individual had the obligation of looking out for his own interests by either avenging himself, or finding a patron who will see to it that the job is done." We who grew up under this code were tested often by authorities including police, teachers, military and most frequent of all, parents. Often, refusing to squeal meant suffering consequences one did not deserve.

At school in the classrooms at Our Lady of Lourdes, we were many boys in a confined space, a situation that created serious potential for mischief, and this was in the day when mischief was simply not tolerated. The teachers and Franciscan Brothers ruled with an iron fist and misbehaving boys did not go unpunished. So when a restless student imitated the sound of a fart, or when an blackboard eraser flew across the room, Brother would turn around slowly and ask the guilty party to step forward. Fat chance since the offender knew this meant the ruler across the hands. And so we all had to write 500 times for homework: "I shall not misbehave in class". If the culprit was known to us he was in for a dose of frontier justice in the cloakroom, but nobody ever ratted him out.

When I was in the army, we had what was called a "Day Room" with a TV set, pool table and writing stations for soldiers who wanted to send letters home. They also had coffee, loose cigarettes and candy, all paid for on the honor system by dropping change in a jar. One day our Sergeant announced that the contents of the jar had been stolen. We had our suspicions, but nobody shared them. Furious, Sergeant Brown had us all dress in full field uniforms including rifles and backpacks, and stand at attention in the hot afternoon sun until the culprit came forward. After someone fainted, our Lieutenant called off the inquisition. He later remarked that he secretly admired our loyalty to one another, which he thought not a bad quality in a soldier.

At my old firm, they had a policy that required any employee who knew about wrongdoing by another to report it under penalty of suspension or termination. The policy was pretty much ignored; like good soldiers and mobsters everywhere, nobody wanted to drop the dime.

Chapter 81:   UNCLE PETE

When I was a kid we lived at 77A Somers Street in Brooklyn. The house was typical for the neighborhood; three stories, a basement and back yard. Our family lived on the first two floors. The "parlor" floor had a kitchen, large living room, a walk-in pantry and bathroom, while the second floor consisted of three railroad-style bedrooms separated by sliding pocket doors. On the third floor was a rental apartment that was occupied by my father's nephew Pete, who I always called Uncle Pete. He was the son of my father's sister Mary, who died at a young age. Lea was Pete's pretty wife, and they had a son, Peter, who lived with them. They also had a daughter, Mary Ellen, who I'm not sure was born to them while they lived with us, or whether she came later after they moved to Ozone Park in Queens.

Uncle Pete came from the large Caruso family that lived a few blocks away on Dean Street. He was the youngest of five brothers including Mike, Johnny, Mario and Jimmy, He also had two sisters, Lucy and Angie. Pete's sisters were two sweethearts who I remember very fondly. His brothers (except for Mike who was quiet and institutionalized for a time), were loud and scary. They drank more than they should, and every time one of them visited, there was usually a squabble. I don't know how he managed it growing up in that house with those brothers, but Uncle Pete turned out to have the sweetest disposition; there was always a smile on his face. He served in the Navy, and after the war got a job as a cook in Kings County Hospital in Brooklyn where his brothers also worked.

I saw a lot of Uncle Pete because he lived right above us. He was always willing to have a catch with me on the sidewalk in front of our house. He also encouraged me to draw. We would sit at my kitchen table and he would sketch pictures of some of the Navy ships on which he served. He was easy to talk to, and not being all that much older than me, felt more like an older brother than an Uncle. His wife Lea had blond hair and movie star good looks. She always had time for me and would ask how things were going at school. I think she might have been my first boyhood crush. Their son Peter was a happy, roly-poly baby who was the apple of their eye. I was sad when Pete and his family moved into their own home because we didn't see as much of them afterward.

After a time, Pete moved his family to Arizona. He had a job opportunity out there, and by then Ozone Park was already changing in terms of the character of the neighborhood. Knowing how much Pete loved his family, I'm sure their safety was a consideration in his decision. For a family of Brooklyn Italians to move to Ozone Park was already a big deal; you can imagine how the move to Arizona must have felt. Ironically, Pete's son Peter, by then a grown young man, was killed tragically in a motorcycle accident not long after the move. His death must have devastated their family, but somehow they picked up the pieces and kept going.

Some years ago, I took a trip to the Grand Canyon with my two sons, and thought I'd pay Uncle Pete a visit. A mutual friend who used to live next door to us on Somers Street had also moved to Arizona, and he arranged for all of us to meet at Pete's daughter's home. I was a little apprehensive when we arrived since it had been so many years that we had seen each other. When we walked in, I saw that familiar smile on Uncle Pete's face and the years just fell away. He gave me a big bear hug and we had a good cry. We went out to dinner, and all night Pete peppered my sons with questions as if he knew he had only one night to learn all he could about them. Lea was as pretty as ever, and we met Mary Ellen's husband and sons.

I found out not too long ago that Uncle Pete had to be placed in a nursing home to be treated for Alzheimer's disease. I'm sure this is very hard on his family, but I hope that somewhere deep down inside him, he recalls drawing with me at the kitchen table, and that this memory brings that familiar and beautiful smile to his face.

Uncle Pete, his wife Leah and me from our Arizona visit

Chapter 82:   UP ON THE ROOF*

"When this old world starts getting me down
And people are just too much for me to face.
I climb way up to the top of the stairs,
And all my cares just drift right into space."

So sang The Drifters in 1962, and in so doing let the world know what every Brooklyn kid already knew: high above the streets it's another world up on the roof. Our family, like many in Brooklyn, lived in a brick, row house with a tiny back yard. I played a lot in my back yard where there really wasn't that much to do, but my imagination made up the difference. I thought I had found my ideal hideaway until one day my father asked me to help with some work he was doing on the roof of our house. I was surprised for two reasons: 1) my father wasn't the handiest guy around; and 2) he had never asked for my help to do *anything*.

Tony Boots (Dad) had decided to re-tar the roof, a smelly, messy business. There were sheets of tar paper and five-gallon drums of sticky black tar that had to be applied with a long, broom-like brush. Dad had trouble getting me to focus on the work because I had never been on our roof before and I was mesmerized by the view. When he took a beer or smoke break, which was often, I would go to the edge of the roof, holler out to my friends, and then duck out of sight while they tried to locate the sound of my voice. I also lobbed small pebbles at them to add to their irritation. My father finally got tired of keeping me from falling, and released me from my roofer's apprenticeship. This was the beginning of my fascination with life up on the roof.

"On the roof, it's peaceful as can be.
And there the world below can't bother me.
Uh oh, up on the roof."

Getting to our roof was impossible; the ladder that led up to the trap door entrance was in the top floor apartment of my house which was occupied by our tenants and cousins, the Carusos. Instead, I would hang out on the apartment house roof where my pal Johnny lived. Access was through a regular door, and open to anyone with the stamina to climb the stairs. Since all the building roofs on the block were adjoining, we could travel the length of the block without setting foot on the sidewalk below. The rooftops were a treasure trove of lost, pink Spaldeen balls hit up there during stickball games in the street. They were a great place to play hide-and-seek too because of the many chimneys and clotheslines up there to hide behind.

In Brooklyn they used to refer to the roof as "tar beach" because people without the time or carfare to go to Coney Island would spread out a blanket on the tar-covered roof to sunbathe. Seeking to avoid contact with the hot, sticky tar, we would "borrow" the beach chairs that people stowed in their hallways because there was no room for them in the small apartments, and take them up to the roof. It was our penthouse club where we drank ice-cold Mission sodas while playing cards and passing around frayed girlie magazines. Urban living doesn't really afford much privacy to kids living in cramped spaced, so the roof became our sanctuary, a private place away from the prying eyes of adults.

"When I come home feelin' tired and beat
I go up where the air is fresh and sweet (up on the roof)
I get away from the hustling crowd
And all that rat-race noise down in the street (up on the roof)
On the roof, the only place I know
Where you just have to wish to make it so
Let's go, up on the roof (up on the roof)"

When you're poor you draw on your wits to create some semblance of the things you can't afford. The old joke about an Italian's idea of a vacation is sitting on someone else's stoop is funny, but also not so far from the truth.

Chapter 83:   The Leprechaun Connection

With St. Patrick's Day around the corner, it got me thinking about the Irish. Some Italian-Americans resent the Irish because of the way they treated immigrants from Italy when they first settled in America. I can't say whether the Irish had any real animosity for Italians, or just viewed them as a threat to their livelihood. The jockeying that goes on to this day when a new wave of immigrants arrives in America is as old as the country itself. New arrivals tend to work for less money in an effort to put down roots and make a living. Just as the Irish were pushed down by English and German immigrants, so the Italians were repressed by the Irish. Usually, over time, each new wave is assimilated, and tensions decrease.

I may be looking at my past through a rose-colored rear view mirror, but I don't recall those feelings of ill will between me and my Irish friends in the neighborhood. Maybe I missed the friction by a generation, but I don't recall my parents harboring such feelings either. My Dad hung out at a place called Grim's Bar under the el on Broadway. The place was owned by the father of New York Yankee pitcher Bob Grim, and had a predominantly Irish clientele. Dad loved his couple of beers after work, and telling his stale jokes to anyone who would listen, even if they were Irishmen. Some of my best friends were Irish, and I always felt welcome in their homes. Our ball games were completely democratic and free of prejudice; if you could play, it didn't matter what your last name was.

Several good people of Irish descent had an influence on my life. One of my closest pals was Richie Bryan. We were in the same class at school, and played on all the same sports teams. Richie's father John was the coach of our baseball team, sponsored by Our Lady of Lourdes. Mr. Bryan not only knew baseball, but he knew kids too. More than once he would pull one of us aside and offer non-baseball advice. He would not tolerate poor sportsmanship or 'hotdogging' on the field, and any kid who tested him on this warmed the bench for a game or two. I don't know what John Bryan did for a living, but he always dressed in a suit, tie and fedora hat, except for our games. He was one of those men who never set out to influence anybody, but by his example, never failed to do so.

I've written before about Lillian Dowd, mother of my friend Tommy, but it seems appropriate to mention her again in this Irish-themed blog. The Dowds lived down the street near the corner of Rockaway Avenue. Because their corner stoop offered a great view of the bustling intersection, we would often sit there and watch the people go by. Sitting on stoops was a major activity in 1950s Brooklyn. Anyhow, most of the women on our block were housewives who dressed in those hideous flowered smocks or house dresses. Not Lillian.

She always wore nice dresses and heels, and smelled of dusting powder. She would frequently ask us to come in and have tea with raisin bread toast. She would make pleasant conversation at her dining room table, covered with an Irish lace table cloth, She talked to us as if we were adults. Her genteel influence helped smooth out our rough edges, almost like a female Professor Henry Higgins tutoring a bunch of male Liza Doolittles.

Finally, there was Father John Schaefer, one of our parish priests. It's safe to say that 12-year old boys are not exactly comfortable in the presence of priests. We were afraid they'd learn our voices and that our anonymity in the confessional would be blown. The priests in our church were nice enough, but never really made an effort to reach out. Father Schaefer was different. Maybe it was because he was younger, and his boyhood days were not that far behind him. Whatever the reason, he seemed to care about us. He was heavily involved in running the school dances held in the church basement, and I once saw him stare down a group of punks from outside the neighborhood who had come looking for trouble. They backed down seeing the resolve in Father Schaefer's eyes. That man did more to keep young boys coming to church than all the other priests combined.

I'm grateful to my Irish friends and all the people who helped influence me for the better. If I could offer a word of advice to young people growing up, it would be to keep your eyes and ears open to such positive influences. God knows there are people who can put you on the wrong path if you let them. Don't shut anybody out of your life because of prejudice; they might be the ones who provide your life-changing moment.

Our Lady of Lourdes baseball coach, John Bryan

Chapter 84:   ERIN GO BRAGH

Speaking of the Irish, a word about St. Patrick, the patron Saint of Ireland. When he became a bishop Patrick dreamed that the Irish were calling him back to Ireland to tell them about God. So he set out for Ireland with the Pope's blessings. There he converted the Gaelic Irish, who were then mostly Pagans, to Christianity. There are many legends associated with St Patrick. It is said that he used the three-leafed shamrock to explain the concept of the Trinity; which refers to the combination of Father, Son, and the Holy Spirit. Legend also has it that Saint Patrick put the curse of God on venomous snakes in Ireland and drove them into the sea where they drowned. Patrick's mission in Ireland lasted for over 20 years. He died on March 17, AD 461. That day has been commemorated as St. Patrick's Day ever since.

As a kid, I grew up in an ethnically mixed neighborhood, but in the church I attended, Our Lady of Lourdes, the dominant influence were the Irish. They had preceded the Italians in the great immigration waves of the late 1800's and early 1900's that deposited so many new inhabitants on our shores. Back then primarily Irish priests presided in Brooklyn parishes and ours was no exception. The laity of our church were mostly Irish too...God fearing people whose pious women starched and ironed priestly vestments and altar linens, and whose red-faced, white-haired men served as ushers and maintenance men. St. Patrick's day was a really big deal for them, and every year the parish hosted a party to celebrate the event in the church basement.

The affair was about what you'd expect. Corned beef and cabbage of course washed down by endless pitchers of beer. I don't believe they served hard liquor but I'm sure many a flask of rye found its way into that low-ceilinged ballroom. The main entertainment at the party was the Lourdes boys' choir, of which I'm proud to say I was a member. We dressed in white shirts, and for this special night, traded our royal blue school ties for ones of bright green. On the makeshift stage, they had set up bleachers of a sort for us to stand on so that we were arranged in rows, with the sopranos up front and the older boys, whose voices were already changing and prone to cracking, hidden in the back rows.

Our choirmaster, Brother Justinian, had rehearsed us well and led us now in song, his stern face topped by jet black hair combed straight back. We sang the Irish classics like: My Wild Irish Rose • I'll Take You Home Again, Kathleen • McNamara's Band • When Irish Eyes Are Smiling • Too-ra-loo-Ra -Loo-ral • Did Your Mother come From Ireland, and our big closer that never failed to reduce all those Irish lads and lassies to tears, Oh Danny Boy. We always received huge ovations, part appreciation for our rousing singing and part relief that the glasses could now be refilled.

We were allowed to stay and enjoy the party for a while, and I learned to my surprise that Brother Justinian had a whole other side to him. This gifted organist and pianist, once lubricated by a few beers, sat down at the piano and brought down the house with everything from pop to classics.

Growing up in Brooklyn, the Irish and Italians didn't always see eye to eye, but I have come to respect them. They are a good people whose migration to America was spurred by hardship and poverty back in the Motherland. I learned more about how grim life in Ireland was from reading marvelous books like "Angela's Ashes" by Frank McCourt. To all my Irish friends, I celebrate you as a people and wish you a happy St. Patrick's Day. For a gift I offer you the old Irish blessing:

"May the road rise to meet you: May the wind be always at your back, The sun shine warm upon your face, The rain fall soft upon your fields, And until we meet again May God hold you in the hollow of his hand."

Chapter 85: IT'S MAGIC

Ed Sullivan used to have a guest on once in a while called The Great Ballantine. He was a comic magician who always cracked me up...kind of a cross between Henny Youngman and David Copperfield who did corny tricks. Some dormant part of my brain kicked in this morning to remind me of how, as a kid growing up, I was fascinated with magic. Every comic book had ads in the back pages for sure fire magic tricks guaranteed to mystify your friends. Some Fifties kids (like Johnny Carson who rode this interest to a successful career) really got hooked on magic. For me it was enough to mystify my friends, who were easily mystified by the way. Here are a few favorites I remember.

Guess the Card - For novice magicians, this was a simple trick involving nothing more than a deck of cards. You would ask a friend to pick a card from the deck, look at it, and replace it face down back in the deck. Of course every magician worth his abracadabra had a little snappy patter to distract the mark so that he would not realize you had cut the deck and looked at the card that would now be on top of his card. You then shuffled the deck and, sifting through it, told your incredulous friend that his card was the ace of spades. The trick was easy to do, and the gimmick not immediately apparent to gullible nine year-olds.

Disappearing Coin Box - This trick involved a wooden box with a pull-out tray containing a cut-out circle where a coin would fit. You would bet your mark that you could make his coin disappear and then reappear. He would put his coin into the slot and then, with a flourish, you would slide the tray back into its recess. After uttering a few magic words, you would slide the tray back out to reveal an empty space where the coin had been. Finally, to allay the look of panic on your friend's face as he saw his nickel disappear, you would slide the empty tray back in, say the magic words, and pull it out again with the precious nickel back in its place. The trick of course was that the box had two trays, but a good magician never gave away his secrets.

The Chinese Handcuffs - Of course everyone today knows the secret of this trick, but back then it was fun to watch a kid struggling to get his fingers out of what looked like an innocent little tube made of straw. The harder they pulled, the tighter the cuffs became. The beauty of this device was its brilliant assumption that when people's fingers are stuck in something, they tend to try to *pull* them apart to get free. Chinese handcuffs were specifically designed to get tighter the harder one tried to pull free. The trick to escape was to *push* the fingers together, at which point the cuffs would give and release the trapped fingers. This was an especially satisfying trick to pull on bigger, stronger kids whose solution to everything was brute force.

The Money Maker - An ingenious contraption that made it appear that the magician could spin straw into gold, or to put it more mundanely, turn blank pieces of paper into money. You would ask the mark if he could use some extra money; the answer was always yes. You would then taks a pre-cut piece of white paper, feed it through the rollers of the Money Maker, and voilà, out came crisp, dollar bills. A variation on this miracle was to feed one dollar bills into the rollers and have five dollar bills come out. The trick was to pre-load the miracle money into the Money Maker so that it was not visible until the crank was turned. The rollers carried the blank paper to an unseen compartment as it rolled out the pre-loaded currency. This trick was always a show stopper.

Magic has come a long way. I get e-mails today showing magic tricks that dazzle and baffle me, but then like my gullible friends of yesteryear, I'm pretty easy to baffle these days.

Chapter 86:   THE FUNNIES

As a kid I was a big fan of the Sunday comics in the newspaper. Many of them like Dick Tracy, Gasoline Alley and Blondie are still around. Looking at them today, they seem to belong to another age and I can't believe they still run them. My father read the New York Journal-American during the week, but on weekends for some reason, he switched to the Daily News. I remember waiting for him to come home from church with the fat Sunday edition of the News under his arm. Before television was part of our lives, the comics section of the newspaper was so popular that New York's Mayor Fiorello LaGuardia used to read them aloud on the radio to kids glued to their Emerson radio consoles.

For adventure, The Phantom was my guy. He lived in the Skull Cave with a trained wolf and rode a big white horse names Hero. Created in 1938 by Lee Falk (who also gave us another favorite of mine called Mandrake the Magician) the Phantom does not have any supernatural powers but instead relies on his strength, intelligence and fearsome reputation of being an immortal ghost to defeat his foes. The Phantom is the 21st in a line of crime fighters that originated in 1536, when the father of British sailor Christopher Walker was killed during a pirate attack. Swearing an oath to fight evil on the skull of his father's murderer, Christopher started the legacy of the Phantom that would be passed from father to son. Cool.

When Charles Schulz sold his first comic strip to the United Feature Syndicate in 1950, it was the Syndicate that changed the name from Li'l Folks to Peanuts - a name that Schulz himself never liked. Hard to believe but Charlie Brown and company have been around for over 60 years. Unlike some of the older strips, Peanuts to me is as funny today as in was back then. The characters are timeless as are Schulz's observations about life. The thing that really put Peanuts over the top for me was the drawings. In a few simple panels, we saw Lucy, Snoopy, Peppermint Patty and all the gang teach us that the world can be cruel. Just as you are about to kick that football through the goalposts, someone just might pull it away.

Dick Tracy, a hard-hitting, fast-shooting and intelligent cop created by Chester Gould made its debut on October 4, 1931. The strip was so popular that it appeared on the front page of most newspaper comics sections. Gould did his best to keep up with the latest in crime fighting techniques; while Tracy's cases often ended in a shootout, he also used new technology and advanced gadgetry like the two-way wrist radio to track down the bad guy. The strip also introduced famous Tracy villains like Pruneface, Mumbles and hitman Flattop Jones. Aided by his partner Sam Ketchum and his sweetheart Tess Trueheart, Dick Tracy was the hero of every law-abiding American boy.

Finally, don't ask me why, I loved Popeye. He first appeared in the daily King Features comic strip Thimble Theatre on January 17, 1929. The strip was created by Pete Segar and revolved around the main characters: Olive Oyl, Popeye's skinny girlfriend, Bluto, Popeye's muscle-headed nemesis, and Popeye's pal Wimpy who would always promise to "...give you a quarter on Tuesday for a hamburger today." The plots were predictable: Olive Oyl flirting with Bluto, panicking when he took her up on it, and Popeye saving the day after eating a can of spinach for strength. Popeye ate spinach in order to encourage children to eat more vegetables; that sure as hell didn't work for me.

It seems like a million years ago when I sat at our kitchen table in Brooklyn, bowl of Cheerios and cup of coffee in front of me, (I didn't have a cigarette with my coffee until I was 12) reading these great old comic strips. The world was simpler then, but life goes on. "Winter must be cold for those with no warm memories." ~From the movie An Affair to Remember

Chapter 87: THE BIRDMAN OF ALCATRAZ

I got to thinking about how panic stricken I used to get as a kid when Labor Day rolled around. When you get to be my age (see "dirt") the months and years whiz by. When you're ten years old, that summer vacation from school felt like it would *never* end. Every day meant you had at least 16 hours to do whatever the hell you pleased...no putting on the school uniform (white shirt and blue tie), no waking up to the alarm clock (strangely, during summer break I often woke before it went off because I couldn't wait to go out to play), and no more pencils, no more books, no more teacher's dirty looks (actually we got a lot more than dirty looks from our teachers if we stepped over the line.)

As the end of the school year approached, I began to feel like the Birdman of Alcatraz waiting for the parole board's decision on whether I could go free. Usually tests were over by mid-June, and the rest of the year was just "make-work" time for kids and teachers until that final bell rang. We had to turn in our text books. God help you if there was so much as a mark on any page. You could plead that it was there when you received the book, but you'd better have a good lawyer or else you were going down. We also had to bring cleaning materials to school to clean up the classrooms. Can you imagine telling a parent today that little Moonbeam or Phoenix (yes, these are real names) would have to scrub desks and wash blackboards!

There was a decidedly lighter air in the classroom on those last few days before summer vacation. Even child-beating teachers would only slap you half-heartedly, as if their minds were already preoccupied with escaping the fifty little demons who made their lives miserable. Lessons per se were dispensed with since report cards were a done deal. Sometimes one of the Franciscan Brothers would tell you a little about their personal life before they entered the religious order. I found these glimpses fascinating because we never thought of them as *having* a personal life; we just assumed they were kidnapped from their parents at an early age and raised in camps where they learned to torment young boys.

The last day of school was the best and the worst. On the one hand, you knew that this was your last day under the gun for two whole months; on the other hand the time passed painfully slowly...today's equivalent for an adult would be like being trapped in an elevator with Nancy Pelosi and Harry Reid. You could smell the summer air coming in the windows since air-conditioning was something you only experienced at the movies. On hot days, the teacher asked a lucky student to take the long wooden pole with the hook at the end, insert the hook into the latch at the top of the tall window, and pull it down a little further. I say lucky because we were such well-indoctrinated Catholic school kids that to us, being asked to pull down the window was considered a *privilege* to be earned.

I know today it is common for kids to take cupcakes and ice cream to school on their birthdays or for an end-of-school party. They even have pizza parties sometimes. This kind of wild revelry was far beyond our imagining. The classroom was a place of *learning*, not for eating treats or other frivolities. Such activities to us would have been comparable to prisoners in solitary confinement at Leavenworth being invited to Hef's Chicago mansion for a Playmate party.

They did allow candy to be sold in the classroom, only because it made money for the school. A student walked up and down the aisles with boxes of chocolate-covered jelly rolls or marshmallow twists and collected a penny or two from the kids who had any money. My friends and I never did, so we just took the candy and threatened to pound the little dweeb in the schoolyard if he ever snitched.

The feeling you got on that first day of summer vacation was unlike any you have as an adult. The closest I ever came was when I called in sick to work and lay in bed watching cartoons all day. Summer in 1950s Brooklyn was special.

Chapter 88:   FREE AT LAST

As the last bell of the school year was ringing, the line of boys in their white shirts and blue ties filed out of Our Lady of Lourdes into the sunlight of freedom. A whole summer to play baseball, swim at Coney Island or Cypress Pool, play punchball, stickball. four-handed Briscola on the stoop...it was enough to make me almost giddy with pleasure. The blue tie came off before I hit the corner of Broadway. Then a right turn up Hull Street, past the firehouse, left on Stone Avenue and right on Somers Street to my house. As I walked, I made sure not to step on any sidewalk cracks; I had my doubts about this superstition, but why take any chances with vacation just beginning.

I hollered to my mother that I was home, as I shot up the stairs, shedding my "good clothes" as I went. I jumped into my summer uniform...dungarees (they only started calling them jeans when the prices went up), white tee shirt with the sleeves rolled up, and U.S. Keds sneakers, black and white, no lights, springs, wheels or any of the other useless crap on sneakers made today. I raced down the stoop into the street as if summer vacation lasted for only one day and I couldn't afford to waste a minute of it. I thought about who I'd *call for*. This is a quaint expression that sounds a little out of place on a Brooklyn street, but that's what we said. "I'll call for you at six" or "I'll be home all day, call for me".

If you had to go someplace, you asked a friend to "walk you". Literally, this sounds like something usually done with a dog, but the term was another example of Brooklyn street talk. "Walk me to Spinners". If your friend refused, you called him a "flat-leaver" or some variation of the phrase, for example, "Alright for you, you flat-leaving bastard!" If you were shooting marbles in the street and there was an obstacle between you and your target, you took a "roundsies" meaning you moved your marble in an arc to the left or right to get a clearer shot. The little carved out hole near the curb that you rolled your marbles into was called the "shimmy". I have no idea how these terms originated; this was the street language of 50s Brooklyn.

During the summer we hit the streets around 8am and began "calling for" our friends. If a lot of guys were around we went up to the vacant lot and started a softball game. The bat was taped, the ball was taped, we had to clear the rocks and broken glass off the base paths, and the bases were made of scraps of cardboard, but we had as much fun as the kids playing today on manicured fields with uniforms and expensive store-bought equipment.

If only a few guys were around, we played punchball, stickball with home plate painted on the wall, triangle, or a game where we threw a Spaldeen ball off the pointed edge of a stoop step for a single-double-triple-or home run, depending on where it landed. After the game we'd head up to Louie's or Sam's Candy Store for freezing cold Mission sodas right out of the red ice chest. Pineapple was my all-time favorite flavor.

The nights were hot. We had no air-conditioners in those days so we stayed out late, usually with our parents keeping vigil from the stoop. To cool off we'd have a Bungalow Bar ice cream or a Popsicle. I had a second floor bedroom and used to sleep with my head out on the window sill for relief. I had to give up this prized spot when my father bought a fan which was placed in the window where my head formerly rested. The fan was a real luxury for us; I felt that, like "The Jeffersons", we were movin' on up. The quintessential example of this poor man's view of the world came from an episode of the old Honeymooners show. Ralph Kramden had found a large sum of cash on the bus (later found to be counterfeit) and was spending like a drunken sailor. Being poor and not knowing how else to spend his windfall, Ralph decided the ultimate in luxury would be to install a phone on the fire escape! Classic.

If you're reading this and thinking we must have felt deprived having as little as we did, you couldn't be more wrong. The reason we didn't feel cheated is that we had no higher standard to compare ourselves to; all the kids I knew were pretty much in the same boat as me. If life gave us lemons, we not only made lemonade, but lemon ice! I know now that a lot of kids had it better than we did back then, but you know what? I'll bet (let's pinky-swear here) that they didn't have as much fun as the kids in my Brooklyn neighborhood.

Chapter 89:   "SPACE HELMET ON, CAPTAIN VIDEO"

To this day I get excited waiting for the mailman. I have no doubt that this feeling of anticipation goes back to the days when, as a kid, I would periodically send away for some gadget or other that one of my radio or TV heroes was urging every fan to get. It usually involved sending in cereal box tops or labels from a sponsor's product. I can't explain to you the fevered excitement that could overcome a ten year old awaiting one of these giveaways to arrive in the mail. The fact that I still remember them more than sixty tears later will give you some idea what they meant to me. When you spied that bulging envelope or small box with your name on it, suddenly all was right with the world.

There was a classic Honeymooners episode when Ed Norton drove Ralph Kramden crazy watching "Captain Video and His Video Rangers". The Captain had a teen aged sidekick who was called The Video Ranger and that's what legions of fans came to be called. *I'm proud to say I was a Video Ranger!* By far the greatest premium offered by Captain Video was a space helmet exactly like the one worn by the Captain himself. It cost a dollar, and it was worth it. A red dome-shaped headpiece was attached to a white plastic piece that encircled the head, and had black earphone-like bulges on the sides. It featured a curved, clear plastic visor, which could be raised for lounging around the Spaceport or lowered for blastoffs. Joining the Video Rangers earned you the coveted membership card which, once you signed your name, bound you to abide by the Code of the Rangers. (If only Bernie Madoff had been a Video Ranger we wouldn't be in this fix!)

The Lone Ranger is one of my all-time heroes. In 1954, I sent away for a Dell two-comic promotional series distributed by Cheerios that told about the origin of the Lone Ranger, how he was saved by his future friend and partner Tonto, why he wears a mask and why he uses silver bullets. I loved the Lone Ranger because he was so unassuming. He always thundered out of town on his magnificent horse Silver before anyone could acclaim his latest good deed. Who can forget the great intro to his TV show: "A fiery horse with the speed of light, a cloud of dust, and a hearty Hi-Yo, Silver! Return with us now to those thrilling days of yesteryear. The Lone Ranger rides again!" I recently checked the price of old Lone Ranger comics on e-bay; sorry Kemo Sabe, no can do.

The original comic strip "Little Orphan Annie" was hugely popular as was the radio show sponsored by Ovaltine. At the end of each radio program, listeners received a secret message that could only be decoded by sending away for the Secret Compartment Decoder Badge. In the 1983 movie "A Christmas Story," little Ralphie finally received his long-awaited Orphan Annie decoder badge in the mail. When he rushed into the bathroom to decode the day's secret message, he was disgusted to find out that it said, "Be Sure To Drink Your Ovaltine." It was funny, to be sure. But it wasn't accurate. Annie's secret messages, which appeared several times each week, were brief previews of what would happen in tomorrow's exciting adventure. That movie was like a time capsule of life in the 1950s, and every time I watch, I love it.
I *was* Ralphie, right down to the burning desire to own a Red Ryder BB gun.

Comic strips in the newspapers were popular in the 1950s. A favorite of mine was Dick Tracy by Chester Gould. Featured in the Tracy strip were Dick's partner with the unlikely name of Sam Catchem, Tess Trueheart, Tracy's girlfriend, and great villains like Pruneface and Flattop. Tracy was one of the first cops to rely on forensic science and advanced gadgets to help track the bad guy down. An example is his great two-way wrist radio, a radical communications concept in its day. Soon ads for the wrist radio appeared proclaiming: "You've seen it in the comics, now you can have one for your very own." Despite my pleas that I would die without a two-way wrist radio, when she heard about the $3.98 price, my mother decided to risk my dying rather than fork over what to her was probably a couple of days worth of grocery money. I checked e-bay...no dice, although a comic book describing the origin of the two-way wrist radio was selling for $299. Thanks a lot Mom.

It takes a lot to impress a kid today. They grow up surrounded by technology, and take it all in stride. How can one communicate to them the thrill we felt as kids at being given the chance to own a secret decoder badge! They would give you that "You poor old man" look that, by the way, I seem to be getting with increasing frequency lately. But I'll bet you dollars to doughnuts (gee, coffee and a doughnut would be nice now) that the fleeting excitement they feel for their latest picture-taking cell phone doesn't come close what we felt in the 1950s on receiving that bulging envelope in the mail.

Chapter 90: RITES OF PASSAGE

Growing up in Brooklyn during the 1950s had its rites of passage. They were different than today to be sure because the world was different. International terrorism was way off in the future, women and minorities were just starting to demand their rights, and the electronic age had yet to descend on an unsuspecting mankind. The view of life from the streets of East New York was decidedly local. Our world was bounded by the streets that defined our neighborhood: Atlantic Avenue to the South, Bushwick Avenue to the North, Pennsylvania Avenue to the East, and Saratoga Avenue to the West. It was a real mix of Irish, Italians, and Germans who had first come over in the great European immigration around the turn of the century, with a few African Americans and Hispanics mixed in.

I guess one of the first steps toward growing up in the neighborhood was the changeover from tricycles to "two-wheelers" as we called them. I have already described how my Dad taught me to ride a two-wheeler. I used to ride a unique looking tricycle that was longer than a standard tricycle with a step on the back that easily carried a standing passenger. It was powder blue and cream colored, with handle bars that were much larger than normal. This thing was a *tank!* I loved riding it, but my friends were stepping up to bigger bikes and it would be unthinkable for me to lag behind.

Another ritual was lighting up your first cigarette. I get a kick out of the way smokers are demonized these days. They have to skulk into dark alleys for a few puffs knowing full well that they are the scourge of decent society. In the 50s, smoking was still cool. All the movie stars, business moguls, athletes, anybody who wanted to look sophisticated was a smoker. I was probably around 11 or 12 when I had my first cigarette. By then my father had switched from unfiltered Lucky Strikes to L&Ms, which were the initials of tobacco manufacturer Liggett & Meyers. Pop used to keep his *butts* as he called them in his suit jacket pocket, so it was an easy matter to snitch one. We would go to Callahan-Kelly park near the handball courts to light up. I remember feeling a little woozy, but dared not show it in front of my friends. At first we just puffed, not yet having mastered the deadly trick of inhaling. I smoked for about 15 years, and stopped when my daughter Laura was born. Thanks Laura.

A big step toward manhood involved scaling the fence behind Spinners, a small supermarket on Fulton Street. Spinners loading dock was in the rear of the store on my block, Somers Street, and was protected by a fifteen foot wrought iron fence. The fence was a formidable affair, anchored on either side to solid brick columns the same height as the fence, and topped by "Stalag 17" quality barbed wire.

During our stickball or punchball games, our pink Spaldeen balls would fly over the fence. The iron fence had sharp points at the top and was clearly un-climbable. The only way to retrieve the balls was to climb one of the brick towers, throw a jacket over the barbed wire, and *gingerly* step over and down the other side. This was a feat greatly admired by kids on my block. I made the climb many times, and owing to my extreme caution, was able to get out with everything I went in with.

Cypress Pool was a shimmering oasis just below the Cypress Hills elevated train station on the Jamaica line. For kids used to swimming in public pools like Betsy Head and Red Hook, this was "movin' on up". Cypress Pool charged 25 cents to keep the riff-raff out. They had three diving boards, a two foot, ten foot and twenty foot. Until you dove off the twenty-foot board, you were *nothing* in the eyes of my crowd. You'd never know it by looking at how timid I've become, but back then no challenge went unanswered. As I climbed that ladder for the first time, waving to the guys below, I felt cocky. When I reached the top platform, second thoughts crept in, but of course I couldn't punk out with everyone looking. I executed a swan dive that saw me enter the water, not vertically, but almost horizontally! Fortunately my friends did not award style points, so I passed the test, with the only consequence being a slightly higher voice for the next half hour or so.

The next rite of passage is one of which I'm not proud. We hung out in Louie's Candy Store under the el on Fulton Street across from the Sportsman's Cafe. Louie and his wife Esther were good to us, letting us sit for hours nursing an egg cream or cherry coke while we played the baseball Home Run machine in back of the store. Some of the kids would dare each other to steal candy from the racks in front of the store. Having never met a dare I didn't like, I accepted. The gang's M.O. was to get Louie to the back of the store while the thief did his dirty work. I'm ashamed to say I pulled many candy jobs at Louie's. I got an adrenaline rush eating the chocolate covered jelly rolls or marshmallow twists I boosted. I wish I could make restitution, but poor trusting Louie is long gone.

I've talked before about how the mind can see clearly events that happened so long ago, while struggling to remember the name of someone you met last week. It's almost as if I can transport myself back to the time when the things I've written about happened. To Richie, Phil, Johnny, Vinny, Lefty, Joe and Tommy...thanks for the dares and for being such a big part of my life.

Tommy, Vinny and Me

Chapter 91: UNPLEASANT MEMORIES

"The victim staggered like a drunk, blood spraying from the ragged wound in the neck where the recently severed head used to be. I stood transfixed in horror, not knowing whether to run or hide. Would I be the next victim?" A scene from "Texas Chainsaw Massacre"? No, just my mother buying a chicken. Back in the days when Frank Perdue was just a gleam in his father's eye, chickens were purchased *fresh killed* at the "chicken market".

If I remember correctly, the market was at the intersection of Pacific Street and East New York Avenue in a run down section of our neighborhood. It was a seedy looking building badly in need of repair. The place stank of burned chicken feathers (that's how they removed the feathers from the dead bird) and your ears were assaulted by the raucous sounds of chickens squawking their heads off as it dawned on them that, well, *their heads were about to come off.* The doomed chickens were kept in pens barely tall enough for them to stand. The customer walked up to this poultry death row, picked out a bird, and the dead-eyed executioner, white apron covered in blood, did the rest. At my insanity hearing, when they try to trace back to the traumatic event in my childhood that first unhinged my mind, the chicken market would be a good place to start.

I am reluctant to mention this next unpleasant childhood memory because it involves me attending an afternoon movie at the Colonial Theater on a day I was supposed to be in school. (My children are chiding me for the admissions of a misspent youth I've already made in this blog.) Anyhow, I was "playing hooky" from high school and sat alone in the dark watching some mid-week B-movie. A man walked down the aisle, and although the theater was nearly empty, entered my row and sat down next to me. I was puzzled of course, but not at all prepared for what happened next. This creep placed his hand on my knee. In a blink I was on my feet and running fast for the door. What annoyed me most was missing the end of the movie.

While attending summer day camp one year, I fractured my left wrist during a high jump competition. I had to go to Kings County Hospital (the medical equivalent of the Roach Motel) to have a hard cast put on from my wrist to my upper arm. The injury happened at the beginning of summer vacation, and required me to wear this itchy cast through the middle of August. What a nightmare: no swimming, no ball playing, and trying to take showers without getting the cast wet. In early August, my family had an outing at some place I can't recall, but I do remember they had a beautiful swimming pool. Watching my cousins splash around on a hot day was more than I could bear.

I grabbed an inner tube and floated around the pool as best I could, despite my mother's protests for me to get out. Unfortunately it was too late. The upper part of the cast got wet and soft, and after visiting the doctor, I had to have a new cast put on and wear it through mid-September. A bummer of a summer.

Mike the butcher had a shop on Rockaway Avenue. His daughter Immaculata (nicknamed "Sis") was one of the girls we tolerated in our all-male, stoop sitting club. Mike was a short, amiable man with no neck and very few teeth. His shop had refrigerated, glass-front counters where his wares would be displayed. Like most butcher shops, the floor was covered with sawdust. Mike had a large, refrigerated back room. Sometimes he would open the big doors and I could see the carcasses of cows, sheep and pigs hanging. Mike would haul one out, lay it on a butcher block table, and start sawing and hacking it into chops, roasts and steaks. This revolted me, and should have turned me into a vegetarian. Happily it did not, and I love a good steak whenever I can get it.

My grandparents lived on Hull Street. My mother would walk us over some afternoons before my grandmother died and the house was sold. I enjoyed these visits since my good friend Rich lived right across the street. What I didn't enjoy was Grandma's basement. I was used to basements (or cellars as we called them) since I played often in our own cellar, especially when it was too cold or wet to go outside. I avoided Grandma's cellar though because it was *creepy*. Like poor people everywhere, to save on the electric bill, they used candles for light down there. The flickering candlelight cast shadows on walls covered with jars of unknown Italian "delicacies" and soda bottles filled with homemade wine. There was junk everywhere...my grandmother was the "handyman" in the family and could do carpentry, plumbing and general fix-it stuff. No spare bit of wood or metal was ever thrown away. I think they filmed the climax scene from "Psycho" down there. The only thing missing was the skeletal remains of Mrs. Bates.

I have mostly pleasant memories from my Brooklyn childhood, but every once in a while I get a flash of recollection reminding me of the things that made me *fraidy-scared*.

Chapter 92:   GET A JOB, SHA NA NA NA NA...

I will always remember my first job. While I was busy carefully weighed career paths worthy of a promising a fourteen-year old, my father found a job for me. He marched me down to the corner and rang the bell of a nondescript storefront with no identifying sign. A man who looked like a Hobbit straight out of Tolkien's imagination answered the ring and invited us in. He introduced himself to me simply as "Mel". I couldn't help notice that Mel walked with a pronounced limp that gave him a rolling gate like Popeye.

Mel asked me whether I could work a few hours a day after school without my grades being affected. I said I could, and after instructing me to report at 4 pm the next day, he hired me for the princely wage of $1.00 an hour. As we walked out it dawned on me that I had no idea what Mel hired me for. I found out the next day that Mel's business was engraving sets of fancy cocktail glasses with people's initials. My job would be to pack the glasses for shipment to his cocktail-drinking customers, whom I imagined all looked like Cary Grant and Myrna Loy.

The "shipping department" was a beat-up, wooden table in a corner of the factory with big bales of straw-like stuff called *excelsior* that was used to pack fragile materials before some genius invented bubble wrap. The main benefit of the job was the collection of eye-catching pinup calendars Mel had hanging on the walls. While gawking at them, it was all I could do to avoid taping my hands together instead of the boxes. The calendars were probably my greatest incentive for showing up to work every day.

Mel turned out to be a quiet, decent man who was a very talented engraver. I did the job for a while, but before long, even the calendars couldn't overcome the mind numbing boredom of packing glasses every day, so I gave Mel my notice. He was really nice about it and even gave me some glasses to take home. They had someone else's initials on them, but still, it was a big step up the glassware ladder for us since we usually drank out of Welch's jelly glasses.

No matter how well off a family is, young people should learn the value of a dollar early in life. Besides teaching me how to pack glasses, that job helped me understand that when I asked my father for ten dollars, it meant the family would have to do without something that week. Starting with my next job, I always gave my mother something out of my earnings for the house. The news story last week of the New Jersey brat who was suing her parents to pay her college tuition is the reason why kids with the entitlement mentality need to learn that there is no money fairy.

Chapter 93: IS IT BIGGER THAN A BREADBOX

Not many around who remember these, but in the days when refrigerators were smaller and people shopped almost daily at local stores, we kept our bread in a bread box. Ours was a cream color with red trim and made of tin with a lid that lifted to get to the bread. There were ventilation holes in the sides to help keep the bread fresh.

Bilello's bread store was around the corner so we bought Italian bread fresh as we needed it. Unlike most modern bakeries, they sold only bread which was baked at their bakery on Pacific Street. The smell was heavenly and the shelves were stocked with warm loaves…round, braided, semolina, seeded…all chewy and delicious. When I was sent to buy a loaf, it rarely arrived home intact.

My mother bought whatever sliced bread was on sale…Wonder, Bond, Taystee or Silvercup are some brands I remember. Sometimes the bakery sold day-old bread or cake and that was always a welcome way to save a few pennies. I remember making PB&J sandwiches with Peter Pan Peanut Butter and Welch's Jelly. When those containers were empty they found new life as our everyday drinking glasses.

Many of us grew up below what would be called the poverty level today but we never thought of ourselves as poor. It was the life we knew, and all our neighbors lived it. Dish night at the movies filled many a china closet, outgrown clothes got handed around, and we picked up deposit bottles for spending money, but I have yet to meet a kid from that era who doesn't speak fondly about their childhood. It was the best of times.

Chapter 94: DOWNTOWN BROOKLYN

In the fifties, we didn't get to Manhattan as much as we did to "Downtown Brooklyn". The downtown section of Brooklyn for us was a major "date" destination. Filled with movie theaters, restaurants and shopping, it was *the* place to go. It's so hard to pick just a few images that represent this unique area. The ones I've chosen are some of my personal favorites such as the iconic Williamsburg Savings Bank, at One Hanson Place, near Atlantic and Flatbush Avenues. It is the tallest building in Brooklyn and its distinctive clock tower could be seen from miles around.

Of all the great movie theaters downtown, maybe the Paramount was best known. A local DJ, Alan Freed, staged rock and roll shows there, and kids lined up for hours to get tickets. Other great theaters in the area were the Fox and Albee, not like the cheesy multiplex venues of today, but extravagant structures with Gothic architecture and opulent, gilded interiors. After the show you could get a bite to eat, and depending on how much you were willing to spend, there were many places from which to choose.

If you thought this date might let you get to second base, you went to a classy place like Junior's. Rightly famous for its cheese cake, Junior's also had good food in pleasant surroundings. It still stands today at Flatbush Avenue and Fulton Street, happily clogging the arteries of new cheesecake aficionados.

If your date fought you off like a tiger in the balcony of the Paramount, then you needed to cut your losses. Maybe doughnuts and coffee at Bickford's Cafeteria on Fulton Street and Fourth Avenue was the place for you. Open 24 hours a day, Bickford's was a popular chain with 48 restaurants, up until the sixties when it slipped into oblivion with the rest of downtown Brooklyn.

Downtown was also a big shopping destination with department stores like Abraham & Strauss, Martin's and Mays. The latter was a lower-end store, but A&S and Martin's were quality establishments. Sales help dressed beautifully, and (just imagine) were required to know the merchandise and actually provide *customer service*.

Today downtown Brooklyn is thriving including big-name stores, rehabilitated subway service and the recently built Atlantic Yards project, new home of the Brooklyn Cyclones basketball team. Condos in the area are going for an incredible $1 million plus in a neighborhood where you couldn't walk safely 20 years ago.

I'm glad its back.

Chapter 95:   DOCTOR IANUCCI

During the late sixties, Doctor shows on television were all the rage. Maybe the most beloved of them all was "Marcus Welby, M.D." If Dr. Welby was a TEN on the Doctor's Rating Scale, then my doctor would have been a ONE. He was the anti-Welby. Dr. Ianucci had his office on Eastern Parkway. His waiting room bore little resemblance to today's spiffy suites. Ratty leather chairs, ash trays full of cigarette butts, faded prints on the walls, and to read, old National Geographics and medical journals....that's what I remember. Not that we got to his office all that much; those were the days when doctors actually made house calls.

If his waiting room could be transformed into a human being, it would look like Dr, Ianucci. He was a rumpled man, probably in his fifties but looked 20 years older. Sagging jowls, a bushy mustache, and slicked-back, iron-grey hair. He dressed professionally in a three-piece suit that that rarely made the trip to the dry-cleaners. I think what I remember most about him most was that he smoked like a chimney; as he examined you, a cigarette with an ash about an inch long always dangled from his mouth, precariously poised and about one puff away from dropping into your pajama top.

The fifties didn't feature many fancy medicines. Penicillin was still being eyed suspiciously. It seems to me today that no matter what ailed you, from migraines to malaria, Dr. Ianucci prescribed Cheracol, a cherry-flavored syrup that could give you a real buzz, or Musterole, an ointment that smelled ungodly, but when rubbed on your chest and covered with a warm flannel cloth probably could cure malaria.

These were the dark days before health care insurance and filling out six forms in triplicate before you got anywhere near the doctor. He didn't send you for five different tests because he was getting a kickback from the labs. There were no gorgeous female drug company reps with cleavage to hand out free TVs to doctors for over prescribing their medications. Dr. Ianucci charged you what you could afford, which I promise you was not much. I'm sure he treated patients who never paid him at all...maybe bring in a bushel of tomatoes from their yard.

As I reflect, I want to revise Dr. Ianucci's rating. Maybe he didn't have a fancy office or miracle drugs, but somehow after one of his visits, you knew you would soon be better. What he brought to the table was a genuine caring attitude for his patients and a brisk, efficient manner that no childhood disease could stand up to. I'm glad he was around to get me through.

Chapter 96: HAROLD BE THY NAME

There's an old joke about a kid who asks his father why God's name is Harold. "What makes you think God's name is Harold", the father asks. Because when we pray the kid answers, we say: "Our Father, who art in Heaven, *Harold* be thy name".

In the Fifties, kids were taught religion by rote...there weren't a lot of explanations. I attended Our Lady of Lourdes in the Bushwick section of Brooklyn. There were many prayers where I didn't understand the words, but we dutifully recited them. Those were the days when the Mass was said in Latin; the lyrics to those Latin hymns were pounded into our heads by Brother Justinian, the choirmaster, and I remember them to this day.

We were required to attend 9 o'clock Mass every Sunday; if you were absent, a note from your parents explaining why was required. We sat with our classmates, and listened for the cue from the nun's "clicker", telling us when to stand, kneel or sit. The nuns patrolled the church aisles looking for kids who were talking, chewing gum, or being otherwise unholy. They were then required to sit in the pew next to the nun for the remainder of the Mass. Most of them didn't *exhale* until they got home.

There were many Catholic rituals that had us gather in the church for elaborate celebrations. The girls were enrolled in "sodalities" dedicated to Mary the Blessed Mother, or to a special Saint. They usually dressed in white, and wore something like laurel wreaths in their hair. From the choir loft where the boy's choir sang, the procession of girls as they marched into church looked like a hedge moving up the aisle.

We also had to go to "Confession" at least once a month. (For non-Catholics, the sacrament of Confession requires that you enter a small, curtained booth, kneel to speak through a screened door opening, and tell your sins to a priest, who then gives you absolution or forgiveness). Being kids from Brooklyn who always looked for an angle, we usually lined up outside the confessional booth of Father Gonzalez who, it was rumored, could not really understand English. It never dawned on us that *God* had no such language problems, and despite the linguistic shortcomings of His representative on earth, would know every dirty little sin we committed.

The Fifties was also the height of the Cold War, and air raid drills were routine. We were huddled into the closet, and told to put our coats over our heads. (Any scientist knows that a corduroy jacket will protect you from A-bomb radiation fallout). My wife tells me that the nuns in her Catholic school were so tough they told the kids that if the Communists ever invaded America, they should *swallow* their miraculous medals. C'mon Commie, you wanna a piece of me.

The Catholic church's Vatican Council II changed a lot of the things about the Mass that I remember from when I was a kid. These changes were supposed to make our religion more "fan friendly". All I know is that in those days, the church was packed to the rafters; not so today. Maybe we need to go in the other direction.

Chapter 97: THE SUBMARINE RACES

It's hard to believe today's headlines that have General Motors teetering on the brink of bankruptcy. There used to be an old saying: "As goes General Motors, so goes the rest of the country". That was certainly true in the 1950s when GM ruled the automotive world. Not only GM, but Ford and Chrysler too owned the American car market. Rising gasoline prices and the arrogance of Detroit executives put Toyota and Honda on the map to stay.

In Brooklyn, your car was an extension of who you were. Any kid over age 12 could tell you the year, make and model of any car that drove by. Cruising around the neighborhood in your souped up Mercury with the windows down and the radio blasting Bill Haley and the Comets was too cool. Steaming up the car windows at the "submarine races" at Plum Beach was a dream date. Gas was cheap and we didn't really have enough money for anything else. Cross Bay Boulevard near the Big Bow-Wow burger joint was where you went drag racing to prove your car was hotter than anyone else's. This lifestyle was captured perfectly in George Lucas' classic film, "American Graffiti". Anyone who saw it knows that George got it right.

Cars gave you the freedom to go to exotic places like drive-in movies. (For you youngsters, this was a huge outdoor theater where you parked your car, hung a speaker on your window, and listened to mediocre movies). Notice I said *"listened"* because if you were lucky, you never got to actually *see* the movie...you were too busy "making out". If you went to the drive-in with just the guys, it was common to put two guys in the trunk of the car to cut down on the price of admission. I remember two drive-ins in particular: The Sunrise Drive-In where we almost always went, and the Whitestone Drive-In where we never went because it was in the friggin' Bronx.

My fantasy car growing up was the 1957 Chevy Bel-Air. It was one of the first really sleek looking cars with awesome fins, not the over-the-top Cadillac fins, but ones that fit the car's proportions and design. And the color had to be aqua. From time to time I watch the Barrett-Jackson classic car auctions on cable TV. They sell lovingly restored cars from the glory years. The audience is filled with guys my age who couldn't afford their fantasy cars when they were younger, and line up to pay through the nose for them now. Needless to say, I plan to stay far away from these auctions.

Chapter 98:   ROCK AROUND THE CLOCK

Popular music in the Fifties was in transition. Big band and swing music was still popular, but the post-war generation was searching for a musical form they could call their own. That search ended in 1954 when Bill Haley and the Comets recorded "Rock Around the Clock". I still wanna boogie whenever I hear that song.

Rock Around the Clock created a sensation when first released, and received additional exposure in the movie of the same name. The film was banned in many countries after reports of teenagers ripping up the theater seats in their excitement over the loud, raucous music on the soundtrack. Rock and Roll was born.

There were so many rock groups in the early days that it would be difficult to name them all. Some were "one-hit-wonders" like The Elegants with their smash recording of "Little Star". They never had another hit. Others had real staying power. I liked The Platters, Dion and the Belmonts, The Diamonds, The Temptations, The Shirelles, The Four Seasons and The Ronettes.

Besides the groups, there were also individual performers whose unique style made them an integral part of the early history of Rock and Roll. Some of my favorites:

Elvis. Perhaps more than anyone, Elvis Presley personifies the definitive rock and roller. His songs and movies of the Fifties and sixties propelled him to the top of the charts. Even after the Beatles and the British invasion of rock, Elvis kept reinventing himself and made comeback after comeback. If I had to pick one person to represent the genre, it would have to be "The King".

Connie Francis. Born Concetta Rosa Maria Franconero in Newark, NJ, Connie's breakout hit was "Who's Sorry Now". That was followed by top sellers including: "Where the Boys Are", "Everybody's Somebody's Fool" and Stupid Cupid". She had such a distinctive sound, and in hit after hit, connected with the teens to the tune of 24 gold albums.

Jerry Lee Lewis. One of early rock's wild men, Jerry Lee burst onto the music scene around 1956 with such piano-pounding hits as "Whole Lotta Shakin' Goin' On" and "Great Balls of Fire". Through a life marked by controversy and personal tragedy, Lewis has remained a defiant figure who refuses to be pigeonholed. Still recording today, he is accorded "icon" status as one of the great rockers of all time.

Little Richard. "A-wop-bom-aloo-mop-a-lop-bam-boom," the famous opening line of "Tutti Frutti" (1955), launched Little Richard's career and remains his signature tune. Along with Elvis, Little Richard, with his slick curls, stiletto-thin mustache, and outrageous behavior helped define early rock and roll. Other memorable hits include "Slippin' and Slidin'," "Long Tall Sally," and "Good Golly Miss Molly."

Johnny Mathis. I couldn't do "fast dances" as a teen, so I prayed for a Johnny Mathis record so that I could get out on the floor. Johnny's romantic ballads like "Wonderful, Wonderful", "It's Not for Me to Say" and his first number one, "Chances Are". With 75 albums and over 100 million records sold, he remains one of my generations favorite performers. On behalf of all the acne-plagued Romeos with two left feet, thanks Johnny.

Roy Orbison. I have a CD of Roy Orbison's Greatest Hits, and it's mind boggling just how many mega-hits this guy put out. Roy had one of the great rock and roll voices: a forceful tenor with amazing range, which he displayed on songs like "Only the Lonely", "Oh! Pretty Woman," "Crying"and "Dream Baby". Sadly, he left us too soon at age 52.

Dick Clark. Many people know Dick (R.I.P.) as the old guy who ushers in the New Year on channel 7. His TV show, "American Bandstand" was *the* venue for new rock and roll artists in the fifties. The show debuted in 1957, and featured Philadelphia teens (who became celebrities in their own rite) dancing in a studio, and guest artists performing their latest songs. Dick was a rock impresario who launched many a career on his show, which lasted into the 1980s.

I love all kinds of music, (except rap) but there will always be a special place in my heart for the unforgettable doo-wop sounds and artists of the Fifties.

Chapter 99:   Minnie and Sal

Minnie and Sal were married to each other, probably because no one else would marry them. I think Minnie may actually have been a distant cousin of my mother from the days when Mom lived in Camden, New Jersey. She always referred to my mother in her drawly, rural Jersey accent as "Cumar Frances". (The word "comare" in Italian was used for the word godmother or a very close friend of the family...then it became a slang term for mistress or lover, as Tony Soprano will gladly tell you.)

Where shall I begin? Minnie was less than five feet tall and more than five feet wide. She had a porcine face with a snout-like nose and innumerable chins, one of which was home to a large, black mole with hairs sprouting out of it. Her hair was worn severely combed back into a tight bun. To complete the picture, she wore rimless glasses that greatly magnified her lifeless brown eyes. Minnie always wore brown dresses....I think it had something to do with a religious sodality to which she belonged. Because of her weight, her legs were always wrapped in ace bandages, and her feet, dainty for her size, were shod in clunky brown shoes that looked like they were taken off a dead Quaker.

Minnie never worked to my knowledge, but she did have a "job" of sorts; she fell down. Once, after slipping on an icy sidewalk, Minnie was hoisted to her feet by the apologetic store owner and offered some cash to forget her mishap. I'm guessing that this incident triggered a miracle of sorts for Minnie, kind of like Bernadette's vision at Lourdes, because after that, she fell down on a regular basis. Every store owner in the neighborhood dreaded the sight of Minnie lumbering down an icy sidewalk toward his store. In a way, her periodic flops did a world of good for everybody in the neighborhood. Because of Minnie, there wasn't an icy sidewalk to be found in all of East New York.

Her husband Sal, or "Goombah Sal" as he was known, was a perfect partner for Minnie. If "Harmony.com" existed back in those days, Sal would have been the one and only match to Minnie's application. Sal was a retired sanitation man. His appearance was striking.... short and stocky in stature, with a dark, swarthy complexion, a hawklike beak for a nose, a full head of jet black hair streaked with grey and a perpetual five-o-clock shadow. His legs were bowed, and he had a rolling gait like a sailor when he walked. He always dressed in a rumpled, ill-fitting suit that looked like he had picked it up along his route before retiring.

He was also partial to bizarre neckties that he fastened to his shirt with not one, but *three* tie-pins. I can still see them like the rungs of a ladder climbing up his shirt....one was in the shape of a sunburst, one was his Holy Name Society pin, and I can't remember the third. One final note about Sal, he insisted on planting a fragrant kiss on my cheek every time he saw me. Now kissing among Italians was not unusual, but Sal *loved* garlic, and his breath could kill a small mammal. I soon learned to duck him. He found it funny, but I knew my very life depended on it.

When Goombah Sal was working his garbage route, he rarely passed up any trash that had life left in it. Their small apartment was strewn with crap. As much as I hated visiting them, I must confess that the curiosity of what I might encounter lying around on the floor was a powerful draw. There were three-legged chairs, assorted pots and pans, single shoes (collecting these completely mystified me unless Sal anticipated losing a leg), broken picture frames, parts of musical instruments...you name it, Sal had it. Since they had no place to store these treasures, they just lived with them like the Collyer Brothers. It wasn't unusual to have to move a toaster with no electric cord before you could sit down.

Minnie and Sal were, shall we say, thrifty. I think they may have originated the custom of leaving the "envelope" empty when they attended a wedding until they saw the quality and quantity of the food and drink. If everything was to their liking, they may have thrown caution to the winds and sprung for a $20 wedding gift. They are also among the few people I have ever seen taking "leftovers" home from a wedding. Sometimes on my birthday, Minnie would glance around to make sure my mother wasn't looking, and then take a quarter wrapped in a tissue and press it into my hand like she was slipping me the Hope Diamond.

Characters were abundant in my old neighborhood. As the old TV show "Naked City" used to say: "There are over 8 million stories in the Naked City". Minnie and Sal were surely one of them.

Chapter 100: SORRY, I HAVE TO RECEIVE IN THE MORNING

Sex on television has gravitated from late-night R movies to prime time. The soaps are full of it at 2 o'clock in the afternoon. Jessica is having Brad's baby even though she feels an unnatural attraction to beautiful Bree, her Pilates teacher. Law and Order: Special Victims Unit often deals with graphic scenes of previously taboo subjects like rape and incest. Janet Jackson has a "wardrobe malfunction" during the Super Bowl half-time show, clearly a lame attempt to spice up her image and breathe life into a career that is so over. You just can't get a break from all the boobs on TV...pun intended.

Then we have the Internet and social media. It seems like every day, some pillar of the community is found with pictures of him having sex with gerbils. How dumb must you be to actually save or email these files! Pornography is rampant; well-meaning parents and school officials try to block these sites, but kids always find a way to access them. I'm convinced that children who are bombarded with sexual images come to have a twisted sense of what sex is supposed to be about.

In the Fifties, this wasn't really a problem. There *was* no Internet, and an ad showing a woman wearing one of those iron maiden bras was enough to get young male pulses racing. Sex on TV was virtually non-existent. In family sitcoms like I Love Lucy, husbands and wives always slept in separate beds. Screen kisses were chaste affairs with no gum-swapping going on. Consequently, it was almost unheard of (despite the wild bragging of guys that knew girls who went *all the way*) for teens to do anything more than kiss on dates.

This wasn't the guys' doing. Men are pigs, and even back in the Fifties, the minute they discovered their sexuality, they were like dogs in heat. Girls were the opposite; their reputations were everything and they guarded them jealously. Starting around 7th or 8th grade, kissing games like Spin the Bottle and Post Office were popular at parties. Most kids, even the girls, participated because there were *rules and boundaries*.

Later there were make-out parties in high school. After a few slow dances to set the mood, couples would pair off and spend hours on couches, porch swings, backyard steps, anywhere they could be alone, making out like mad.

At the stage when things were ready to move to the next level, the girl would firmly push away and say something like" Sorry Skippy, not tonight. I have to *receive* in the morning". (For non-Catholics, this meant she had to receive Communion at morning Mass.) The dopey guy, who deep down knew this would be the inevitable ending, nevertheless allowed himself to dream about what was under that pink angora sweater. When reality dawned, he limped home for the all-to-familiar cold shower.

When I think about how innocent we were back then compared to teens today who grow up so fast (at least where sex is concerned) I think I like the old way better. "The dance" was a lot slower and there was no unspoken rule about sex by the third date. In spite of all the cold showers, I like to believe that we had more respect for women. It's an old-fashioned notion, and maybe I'm remembering things as being better than they were, but I'd rather see a woman up on a pedestal than hanging off a brass pole.

Chapter 101: THE EASTER SQUIRREL

With Palm Sunday and Easter around the corner, I'm reminded of things about these holidays that connect me to my childhood.

In my old neighborhood, Palm Sunday was kind of the warm-up act for Easter. In church they handed out palm to commemorate Jesus' ride into Jerusalem and how the people there lay down small palm branches in his path. Somehow the religious symbolism of the palm leaves got lost in our church. Old Italian women dressed in regulation black dresses jockeyed for aisle seats where they could grab as much palm as possible before passing the remaining few scraggly strands down the pew. Most of them had no earthly use for it, but that didn't matter as long as they got more than anyone else. Every Italian-American home had palm crosses hanging somewhere until Labor Day.

The week before Easter Sunday is a holy time. On Holy Thursday we visited different churches. It was customary for churches to cover up all the religious statues during Lent. It looked as if they were getting ready to move. One thing I remember is my mother dragging me to Klein's Department Store in Union Square to shop for my Easter suit and good shoes. Families dressed up for Easter Sunday back then, including one year when nearly every guy in church wore charcoal grey and pink, as if by Papal Decree. Being a thrifty woman, my mom always bought clothes that were a "little big" for me so I could grow into them. Sixty years later, I still haven't grown into my Confirmation suit.

In ancient times eggs were dyed for spring festivals. In medieval Europe, beautifully decorated eggs were given as gifts. Carl Faberge, the world-famous goldsmith and jeweler to the Tsars of Russia, created some fabulous eggs that today are renown for their beauty. We continue this tradition today at Easter. Those old egg decorating kits never changed: small swatches of dye to color the water, and those little transfer decals of chicks and bunnies that invariably *shredded* when you tried to apply them. These colored eggs were also used to make a braided Easter bread that I think was called Pane di Pasqua. Nobody in my family ate it so I had the whole loaf to myself, thank you.

I recall too, certain movies being shown around Easter like Irving Berlin's "Easter Parade", with Fred Astaire and Judy Garland; The Ten Commandments with Charlton Heston, Yul Brenner, and the horribly miscast Edward G. Robinson snarling at the downtrodden Jewish people: "Where's your Moses now?!" And "The Greatest Story Ever Told" with Max Von Sydow as Jesus. My wife says she used go see a silent version of "King of Kings" every Easter season at the Plaza Theater in Brooklyn. Her parochial school gave the kids a five-cent coupon that reduced the price of admission to twenty cents. Finally, for some bizarre reason, Channel 9 in NYC always showed that sacred Easter classic, "King Kong."

I connect certain foods, especially treats, to the season of Easter. Yellow marshmallow chicks, milk-chocolate bunnies and of course jelly beans (blacks are my favorite). My aunts would make Easter pies, struffoli (honey balls) pizza grana, ricotta pie and of course the lamb-shaped cake. My poor mother tried to keep candy in the house for her Easter guests, but had to find ingenious places to hide it. I could sniff out a piece of chocolate like a pig sniffs out truffles. I remember once hitting pay dirt when I tracked down a solid chocolate bunny concealed in an innocent basket of folded laundry. My mother went nuts when she went to retrieve it on Easter Sunday only to find that its ears had mysteriously gone missing, and it looked more like the *Easter Squirrel*.

Funny how the memory works. Short-term memory (did I put on underwear this morning?) tends to weaken, but long-term memory somehow remains strong, as if to keep you mentally connected to who you are and where you came from. I'm very thankful for this.

My daughter Laura in her Easter finery, circa early 1970s

Chapter 102: LIFE IN THE STREET

1950's Brooklyn was a community that lived in the streets.

As soon as we got home from school, or at sunrise on weekends, boys were in the street. There was no problem finding playmates, and even if there was nobody around, we just rang a few bells. Our games were physical and involved running, climbing and jumping…childhood obesity was rare. We dodged cars playing stickball or punch ball, roller skated and rode our bikes or sleds in the street. Lost Spaldeens were retrieved from rooftops or sewers without a thought of danger or germs. Open Johnny pumps were our swimming hole. At night we played under the streetlights until we heard our mothers called us home under penalty of death.

Girls were right there too. They played "A my name is Anna" or jumped rope, double Dutch style while chanting their sing-song accompaniment. Jacks was a game that boys and girls sometimes played together, and doll carriages were paraded up and down the block. The more athletic girls wanted to prove they could compete with boys and many did. As we got older there was more socializing between boys and girls. Basement birthday parties often evolved into kissing games like Spin the Bottle and Post Office. This was in the days before rampant promiscuity, and so the nights usually ended in cold showers.

Men sat outside social clubs pitching pennies, playing cards and sipping espresso or listening to the ball game on a transistor radio with cold cans of Rhinegold or Schaeffer beer in their hands. Older men took up their duty of hosing down stoops and sidewalks. They looked innocent enough, but if a stranger walked onto the block, the old men would go into interrogation mode: Who are you looking for? Do you live around here? No newcomer passed unchallenged. When a pretty girl passed the old men would tip their caps and make flirtatious small talk. It reminded them of their chivalrous younger days.

Women were outside as well, walking to local stores with a shopping cart to buy a few days groceries. There were no big box stores or giant refrigerators then and everything was bought fresh. At night they sat on stoops to cool off after a long day of cooking and cleaning. They shared a bit of gossip while waiting for the ice cream man to show up. Older women also served in the neighborhood watch, sitting at their posts in second or third floor windows. They were the eyes and ears of neighborhood mothers, and delighted in ratting out kids they caught sneaking a smoke or dropping an F bomb.

This was the life in any 1950's Brooklyn neighborhood you could name. It doesn't seem like much, but was a great character builder and teacher of street smarts not learnable elsewhere. Problems, yes. Perfect, no. But I loved every minute.

Our neighbor, Loretta, could swing a mean bat

Chapter 103:   GROWING UP

As kids we sometimes talked about what we would become when we grew to adulthood. Most of us had no clue. It's amazing when you think about it that such an important decision was given so little thought. We all knew we had to go to high school, but after that, who knew? Few families in the neighborhood could afford college for their children. Most were counting the days until kids living at home could get jobs and start helping out with the expenses. Girls with no special calling thought about being secretaries or working as telephone operators. For the guys it was either a laborer or an office job. We did have some cops, firemen, teachers and nurses, but most of us just drifted into any job we could get.

Today, high schools have counselors and college recruiters to help seniors decide on a career. When I went to high school, if you saw the guidance counselor, it usually meant you were in trouble. I attended Brooklyn Tech, considered a very good school then and now. The first two years of study were general academics, but starting in junior year, students selected a tailored course of study to prepare them either for college or a job. Some of the specialized tracks included Electrical, Chemical, Mechanical, Structural and Architectural. I picked Industrial Design because I loved to draw and I was good at it. Unfortunately not enough juniors chose that track and so Tech did not offer it that year. I wound up in the Aeronautical track, God knows why, and I hated it. I was turned off to school and scraped through my remaining high school years.

My first job out of high school was for Bankers Trust Company on 46th Street in Manhattan. The pay was a fast $52 bucks a week, but they gave every employee a free checking account. I thought I died and went to heaven. The part about a checking account that did not sink into my teenage brain was the need to actually have money in the account before writing the checks. I think some of the checks I wrote back then are still bouncing. The job was boring but I met a bunch of guys that became good friends. We could be found most Friday nights in Johnny's Bar across the street blowing off the pressures of the week and trying to impress girls; we rarely succeeded.

Thanks to a tip from a neighborhood friend, I applied for a job with the Standard Register Company based in Dayton, Ohio. They sold business forms and equipment, and had an opening for a forms designer. The drawing skills I had honed at Brooklyn Tech came in very handy, and I got the job. I later went into sales and worked out of their office in Roslyn, Long Island. I recently received a call from a co-worker of mine at Standard Register named Mike Giorgio. He says he was just calling around to try to locate some old friends and wants to have a drink. I liked Mike and will join him for a drink...I'm just suspicious that he's got some pyramid scheme going and is looking for victims. That's me, glass half empty.

I soon realized that the jobs I was working were dead end, and with a nudge from my wife, started evening college classes. Eventually I got a Masters Degree in Business Administration from Bernard Baruch College back in the days when you needed more than just a pulse to graduate. I had a very satisfying career with Con Edison, and have worked as a part-time consultant for them since I retired ten years ago.

I sometimes wonder what turn my life would have taken if I had completed the Industrial Design study track back at Brooklyn Tech. We like to think we have control over our lives, but more often than not, some chance event alters our fate and there is no going back. All in all, no complaints.

Chapter 104: BRING BACK "OLD SCHOOL"

Sad to say, but "old school" is in decline. Some might think this is a good thing, but it's not. To me, when you say someone is "old school", that isn't a pejorative but rather the highest compliment that can be paid. Old school means doing things the right way, even when it may not be fashionable. Old school means having principles and sticking by them. It means no shortcuts, not being afraid to follow your conscience, not worrying about being popular, and no apologies. Old-schoolers believe in family, God and country. They believe in education for its own sake. Hard work is what they know, and they are not tolerant of laziness. They are respectful and polite to others in an increasingly hostile world.

I grew up in an old school world where there was little tolerance for self-pity and no professional victims who blamed everyone for their problems except themselves. If you wanted to eat and have a roof over your head, you worked. As I think back, many of the jobs people did were hard. There were still ice boxes around in those days. Before electric refrigeration people used wooden boxes that held blocks of ice to keep food from spoiling. These blocks were delivered by muscular men who drove trucks and delivered the ice blocks from the ice house to their destinations. I remember they wore burlap sacks over the shoulder onto which they hefted the heavy blocks using a large metal pincers. Oftentimes they delivered to second or third floor apartments. The work was brutal, but they did it with dignity. This is how they fed their families. They were old school.

For many neighborhood people, education was something of a luxury. They had to quit school and go to work to help out the family. It's no wonder that they vowed their kids would not suffer the same fate. Many dipped into meager incomes and found the few dollars to send their children to parochial schools. Others relied on the public schools which were exceptional in those days. Kids were encouraged to learn and parents allowed the schools to do their jobs without the incessant interference teachers must put up with today. At graduations, you would see these old school parents bursting with pride as their sons or daughters received their diplomas. Having a college grad in the family was almost unheard of. For them, an education was everything. They were old school.

Being poor was no excuse for being rude. There were standards, and people abided by them. You respected your mother and father, not only because the ten commandments required it but because it was the right thing to do. You respected elders and people in authority like policemen, clergymen and teachers. Men held doors for women; young people gave up their seats on the bus to older people; profanity in mixed company was looked down on; manners were actually something we cared about. I remember learning things in school like how to make a proper social introduction, how to act at the dinner table; not to stare at people who were different; and how the words "please", "sorry", and thank you" could take you a long way in this world.
Courtesy is old school.

Clearly attitudes about things like work, education, and family have changed over the years. I see kids saying things to their parents and teachers that would have got me a wooden spoon upside my head. I see punks taunting cops and the cops bending over backwards to avoid responding. An old school cop would have planted his foot in someone's ass and administered a much needed lesson. Teachers get hassled by bratty kids with no manners and no fear of reprisals because they know Mommy will back them up. Bullies electronically terrorize the odd kid out until the poor kid does something to himself or someone else. This is the world we live in and I think we are all worse off for it. We could use a little "old school" to turn things around.

Chapter 105: LOOKING BACK

If I had to pick a decade to spend the rest of my life in, it would be the 1950s. I know what you're thinking, another old coot looking for his lost youth, but it's more than that. Life in America was different then. Americans were different too. There was optimism in the air. People still believed the Horatio Alger stories where the main character, Ragged Dick, (hey, I didn't name him) overcame poverty by working hard and leading an exemplary life, eventually gaining wealth and honor. Those stories may have been exaggerated some, but Americans generally felt that if they got an education, paid their dues, and worked hard, they would succeed. And they did for the most part without welfare, food stamps or government handouts.

Family roles were clearly defined. The men went to work and the women stayed home, kept house and cared for the kids. This model of the American family served the country well for a hundred years. And in case we needed examples to show us the way, we had "Father Knows Best", "The Ozzie and Harriet Show" and "The Donna Reed Show" as templates for what a family should be. Mothers rarely worked, kids didn't go to school until kindergarten, and when they got home, Mom was waiting with milk and cookies to help with homework. There were no nannies to care for the children; that was Mom's job. On weekends, Dad puttered around the house or took the kids out to learn how to ride a bike or hit a baseball.

The United States was the envy of the world. Our economy was strong, jobs were plentiful, and anything 'American' was soon being copied by the rest of the world. Literature, art, entertainment, commerce, science and medicine were reaching new heights. American might was respected and feared all over the globe. If we went to war, our young men were ready to defend their country. They understood that our way of life was only as safe as our military might made it. There were no anti-war protests, women were not setting their bras on fire, school administrators maintained order and discipline without drugging our kids and cops were given a wide berth if you knew what was good for you.

Technology had not yet become an addiction for our citizens. People spoke face-to-face or, if you were lucky enough to have one, on the big black telephone sitting in the living room. Kids played outside instead of sticking their faces in a computer or video game. The pressure for material things did not drive our existence. Clothes and toys got handed down without shame, cars and appliances got fixed instead of junked, we had one TV and we gathered around to watch as a family rather than hiding in our rooms and surfing the net, easy prey to perverts who prowl the chat rooms looking for vulnerable kids with something missing in their lives.

If you got sick, the doctor came to the house and healed you for five dollars. There were no massive HMOs with their forms in triplicate, or money-hungry doctors looking to put another Cadillac in their garages. We didn't use heroin, crack or cocaine; I think Cherecol cough syrup was the strongest drug I ever took. Hypertension and clinical depression were not epidemic, there was no AIDS and psychiatrists needed second jobs to make a living. We ate what we enjoyed, and strangely enough, all those beans, lentils and greens we ate because that was all we could afford turned out to be the secret to good health. We didn't know what cholesterol was and ate ice cream and cannolis without guilt.

I know there were problems. Race relations were horrible. We still went to war. Women and minorities battled the glass ceiling. But are we that much better off now? Race relations seem worse than ever, only now we have added guns to the mix. We are at war today with an unseen enemy who will not meet us on the battlefield but instead kills us by flying planes into buildings and strapping bombs to their children. The basic family unit is under attack. Unemployment and the entitlement mentality are rampant. Divorce and child abuse are at all time highs. Our leaders are in office, not because of their ability to govern, but because they can make pretty speeches. Our own citizens and countries around the world are losing confidence in America. People live in fear of the unknown.

Honestly, you can keep your 60 years of progress and drop me back into the middle of 1955. I'll be just fine, thanks.

EPILOGUE

It's funny how the memory works. As we get older, it seems that long term memory improves. That has certainly been the case for me. The things I've written about growing up in Brooklyn are so vivid it feels like they happened yesterday, but alas, time has marched merrily along.

I'm betting that a lot of people who get to be my age (going on 76 at this writing) sit down at some point and take stock of their lives. Is the world any different because of me? What will I be remembered for? For most of us those are not easy questions to answer.

We want to think our lives mattered. Maybe we didn't save peoples' lives like doctors and nurses, or risk our personal safety to protect others like police officers and fire fighters. Like teachers, did we light a spark in a child's life that led to great things or console the bereaved and provide spiritual guidance like people of the church?

I'd like to think that all lives matter. If you've ever seen one of my favorite movies: "It's a Wonderful Life" you'll know that this was the message of that movie. On the brink of suicide, George Bailey, the film's main character, is reminded by his guardian angel of the lives he touched to make them better.

Growing up in Brooklyn, I never fully appreciated the lives that touched mine. Parents, siblings, extended family members, teachers, coaches, so many people schooled me in how to do the right thing and for them I will be forever grateful. I hope my time here has made a difference. There is one contribution to the world of which I couldn't be prouder…our children, Laura, Michael and Matthew.

They have surely made the world a better place by being in it. I tried to raise them with the common-sense Brooklyn values that guide me to this day. Family comes first. Respect people unless they give you reason to do otherwise. Always do something to the best of your ability. Never take living in America for granted. Make time for God.

I hope you have enjoyed reading this book as much as I've enjoyed writing it. I was astounded to learn how many people out there were raised as I was and enjoy the same memories. No matter where we are, we will always be from Brooklyn.

My contribution to a better world…Laura, Mike and Matt

Laura, Ava and Malcolm

Tara, James and Mike

Alicia, Priscilla and Matt

75237118R00130

Made in the USA
Middletown, DE
04 June 2018